The Spirit of the New Silk Road

EIR Contents

www.larouchepub.com   Volume 45, Number 13, March 30, 2018

Schiller Institute

I. From the New World

The Belt and Road Vision: To Create A Mass Movement for Development

by Helga Zepp-LaRouche

Zepp-LaRouche delivered this keynote address to a March 22 Spanish-language EIR *Schiller Institute international webcast, which included live audiences in Lima, Peru; Mexico City; and Hermosillo, Mexico. It was pre-recorded March 19. The transcript has been edited.*

Hello to all of you participating in this conference!

The New Silk Road Spirit is a very powerful new dynamic in the world. As a matter of fact, it is already the dominating tendency of the whole globe, in which 140 countries are already participating. Not everyone is happy to cooperate with this new paradigm, however. There is a very strong, almost violent opposition coming from those who are defending the old, geopolitical, unipolar world order. As a matter of fact, they are proceeding from the axiomatic assumption that everything that is associated with the unipolar world, with the Pax Britannica, or the Pax Americana, is good; that liberal democracy and human rights protections are inherently good, while Russia, China, infrastructure, and credit-issuance without strings attached, are bad.

You can see by the events unfolding over the recent days and weeks, that there is an incredible double standard, where those people who pretend to uphold all the good values are, indeed, precisely the ones who are creating havoc in the world. The best example—or not the best example maybe, but the most horrible, is what Theresa May, the Prime Minister of Great Britain, just did in the case of the so-called double agent Sergei Skripal, who was attacked with a nerve agent. Without delivering any proof, May gave an ultimatum to Russia, demanding that within 24 hours Russia must provide evidence on how this nerve agent came into Great Britain.

Some experts doubt that this nerve agent even exists, and strongly doubt that the British have any sample to compare it with. Nor did the British follow the protocols of the Organization for the Prohibition of Chemical Weapons (OPCW), which require that Britain furnish a sample of the nerve agent to this organization and to Russia, with the accused country—namely Russia—having ten days to respond.

What Theresa May did instead, was create, in a single day, something which you could only call a war-time, or pre-war alliance, consisting of Angela Merkel, the Chancellor of Germany; Emmanuel Macron, the President of France; and herself. She tried but failed to pull in President Trump, who initially was very reluctant to say that this was clearly the Russians.

VIDEO: Theresa May: Russia highly likely to be behind poisoning (ABC News)

It is "highly likely" Russia was responsible for poisoning ex-spy Sergei Skripal with a military-grade nerve agent in south-western England last week, Britain's Prime Minister, Theresa

RELATED STORY: Hundreds told to 'wash' your clothes, wipe your phones' after nerve agent attack

RELATED STORY: Son's grave scoured for clues into nerve gas attack on Russian double agent

Craig Murray, a former British ambassador to Uzbekistan, denounced all this, pointing to the fact that it follows the same script which was used in 2003, declaring there were "weapons of mass destruction" in the hands of Saddam Hussein, which was the pretext for the Iraq War. And as we remember, this script came from the MI6, the foreign intelligence agency of the British. As we know, that hoax led to a terrible catastrophe. Millions of people died in the aftermath of the wars against Iraq, Libya, and Syria. Therefore, this present accusation can only be seen as pre-war propaganda, leading possibly to a nuclear showdown with Russia, or at least risking that.

When Russia did not immediately respond to the ultimatum, the British expelled 23 Russian diplomats. Maria Zakharova, spokeswoman for the Russian Foreign Ministry, characterized May's stunt not as an "incident" but a full-blown "international provocation." The British never apologized for the lies and the consequences of the so-called weapons of mass destruction in Iraq, she said, but only "apologized" for having misspent some money from the British budget. Such an apology can never make up for the terrible destruction of the entire Middle East, and the resulting refugee crisis which has wreaked such havoc since.

In the aftermath of the Skirpal affair, the Russian Defense Ministry announced that a Russian nuclear submarine squadron had just concluded a stealth exercise off the coast of the United States, proving that it can approach the shores of the United States without being detected. This comes immediately after a very dramatic, televised speech of President Putin, delivered to the Russian Federal Assembly on March 1. He announced that, as a consequence of the United States unilaterally cancelling the ABM Treaty in 2002, Russia had no other recourse—given the fact that all Russia's proposals for disarmament or a new security architecture went unanswered—but to rely on the creativity of the Russian scientists and military, who developed new systems, including a highly maneuverable, very fast rocket, moving at Mach 20, which renders the U.S. anti-ballistic missile system obsolete. He also announced a nuclear-powered undersea drone, which is not only a severe threat to the aircraft carriers, but totally changes the strategic balance which had been altered by the U.S. ABM systems.

I've mentioned these things to show you that we are

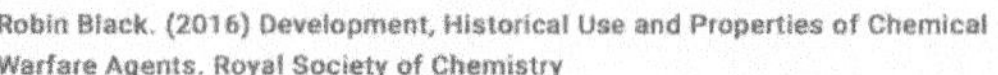

really in an extremely dangerous situation, and to help you understand why this renewed Cold War—threatening to possibly become a hot war—is happening. At a recent forum in Moscow, Russian Foreign Minister Sergey Lavrov stated that the United States and the West in general are very nervous about the comeback of Russia as an equal partner, proving that Obama's characterization of Russia as a mere regional power is completely wrong. He said that Russia does not intend to have a confrontation with anybody, but that 500 years of Western domination of world affairs is coming to an end and that the transition to a new, multipolar world—which will be democratic, just, and based on a new paradigm—will take quite a while to be completed, but even the prospect of such a change in the world order is very painful for those who are in the habit of running the world.

I think that is what westerners are witnessing right now: the collapse of the old order, based on neo-liberal conceptions based on geopolitics, and the very, very rapid emergence of a completely new paradigm.

It is quite amazing. President Xi Jinping announced the New Silk Road in Kazakhstan in September 2013, only four and a half years ago. But in these four and half years, this project has developed very, very quickly, and is already the largest infrastructure project in history, somewhere between 12 and 20 times as big as the post-World War II Marshall Plan, but without the military connotations.

For four years, there was almost no coverage in the mainstream media! It's unbelievable: here you have the largest development and industrialization program in

Xinhua

Coca Codo Sinclair hydroelectric power plant, located about 150 kilometers east of Quito, was built by China's Sinohydro consortium. The power plant, the largest facility of its kind in the country, is expected to supply 30 percent of Ecuador's electricity needs.

history, and the Western mainstream media don't find it newsworthy enough to report? Does this have something to do with the arrogance of power of those who have been used to running the world?

Recently, when the total success of this project became so overwhelmingly obvious, there was a sudden series of attacks coming from think tanks, from the Center for Strategic and International Studies in Washington, from the European Council on Foreign Relations, and from the Mercator Institute for China Studies think tank in Berlin. Some claimed the New Silk Road to be a threat to the liberal system, to liberal values. Before leaving for a tour of Latin America, then Secretary of State Rex Tillerson declared that Latin America doesn't need the new imperialism—meaning alleged Chinese imperialism. He did the same thing in Africa, by the way. And then, Admiral Kurt Tidd, Commander of the U.S. Southern Command, chimed in, saying that China is making aggressive investments in Central and South America.

If you think that what China is doing in Latin America is "aggressive investment," you obviously have geopolitical glasses on your nose, so you have a distorted view of reality.

Face the Reality of Today

The reality is very different. China is an amazing country. I say this with a little pride. I don't claim to be a China expert, but I've looked closely at China and been very involved with China since 1971, when I was there for the first time, during the Cultural Revolution.

The development that China has undergone during the last 40 years, since the reforms of Deng Xiaoping, is the most amazing example of human creativity and the determination to change the fate of society for the better.

China has lifted 700 million people out of poverty; it has a booming economy, which is very healthy, contrary to all the reports in the West; and what Xi Jinping presented at the 19th National Congress of the Communist Party of China last October, is the only vision for the future for the next 30, 40, and 50 years. He proclaimed that China will have eliminated all poverty at home by 2020. That's only two years from now; 30 million people in China are still regarded as poor. There are *tremendous* programs right now, in which party members are going into the villages, investigating on a case-by-cases basis, as to why each particular individual is poor; bringing in infrastructure, education for the children, and providing farmers with access to e-commerce, so they can sell their products in a modern way. So, it is absolutely believable that China will reach the goal of eliminating domestic poverty by 2020.

By 2025, China wants to be the vanguard in several scientific fields. China is already the leader in high-speed rail systems, producing the most efficient, and the greatest extent of high-speed rail systems in the world. At the recent party conference, they discussed a new maglev system, which will travel at 600 kph, and a new underground tube system at 1,000 kph. A fast maglev system for inner-city transportation will travel at 160 kph. The fact that maglev technology provides extremely quick acceleration, and can reach maximum

speed in almost no time, makes maglev trains extremely effective for urban transportation.

The other goal is that by 2035, China will be a modern, democratic country with socialism with Chinese characteristics. And by the year 2050, China will be a fully modernized, strong country, democratic and culturally advanced, whose people have beautiful lives and pursue their happiness. Xi Jinping said it was the aim of China to not only provide that for the Chinese people, but for all nations of this world.

The Belt and Road Initiative is obviously in the tradition of the ancient Silk Road. As that old Silk Road exchanged culture, ideas, technologies, and goods, so does the New Silk Road. Especially, it offers a new model for economic development to the other developing countries, and it provides credit to address the huge gap in infrastructure and industrial funding which was left by the IMF and the World Bank. As you know, those two institutions had, and still impose certain "conditionalities," which oblige the borrowing, i.e., debt-incurring countries, to cut all social programs and slash infrastructure spending, making it impossible for them to repay the debt. And while the mainstream media accuse China of luring developing countries into a debt trap, the opposite is true! Because, as John Perkins wrote in his very worthwhile book, *Confessions of an Economic Hit Man*, it was the deliberate policy of institutions like the World Bank and the IMF to *cause* an unpayable debt trap for the developing countries, and to impose conditions that would mean absolutely no de-

velopment. If you want to know why the developing countries are in such an undeveloped condition, it has something to do with these institutions.

Adjunct Associate Prof. Friedrich Wu, of the S. Rajaratnam School of International Studies at Nanyang Technological University in Singapore, pointed in a recent article, to a study by the AidData laboratory at the College of William and Mary in the United States, which shows that four-fifths of the recent years' Chinese lending was on concessional terms, i.e., below market interest-rates. Professor Wu also quotes David Dollar of the Brookings Institution, who finds that China has been lending without any discrimination in regard to "geography or the quality of governance," which proves this is a "demand-driven" pattern, rather than a "supply-driven development" guided "by a Chinese master plan."

Additionally, the Asian Infrastructure Investment Bank (AIIB)—first proposed by China, but now counting 60 other members as well—has shown a complete absence of any political agenda in the loans it has made in its first two years of development financing. So anyone who says that China is pursuing a master plan, and pursuing its own exclusive interests, is readily proven wrong by the reality of the Silk Road and the AIIB. Rather, China is engaging in win-win cooperation, with complete respect for the sovereignty of the partner nation, complete respect for its social system, and no interference and no effort to try to change that system. And that has everything to do with the fact that, while the Chinese say that they have a socialist country with Chinese characteristics, I always think—and say—that the "Chinese characteristic" is the 2,500-year-old Confucian tradition, with its notion of the harmonious development of different cultures.

Confucianism, unlike Christianity, for example, does not proselytize and attempt to recruit other people to Confucianism. It is perfectly happy if there is the development of all. Xi Jinping calls this the "shared community for the future of humanity," which I think is exactly truthful.

The New Silk Road Spirit is spreading so fast, because countries realize that it is in their self-interest to cooperate. It's spreading in Asia, and it is even spreading to Europe. The Eastern and Central European countries, the 16+1 countries, are fully on board. The Balkan countries are absolutely happy about China's investments. So is Italy, and so are Spain and Portugal, which not only want to be the western end of the Silk Road in

Xinhua/Chen Cheng

Mazeras railroad bridge built in Kenya after a 2014 deal with China.

Eurasia, but also want to be the hub for trade and development with the Latin American countries and the Portuguese-speaking countries in Africa. Even Switzerland, Netherlands, Belgium, and Austria are joining. In Austria, the new government has even put cooperation with the Silk Road in its government coalition agreement. The only countries putting on the brakes are Britain and Germany, as is the EU headquarters in Brussels.

Now the most incredible and most exciting example of the transformation brought about by the New Silk Road comes from Africa. A railroad is now functioning between Djibouti and Addis Ababa, a distance of 750 km; new rail lines are being built in Kenya, Cameroon, and Rwanda, with others in preparation. Many industrial parks are being built, and new hydropower is being planned and provided. There is a completely new spirit of optimism in Africa, which did not exist under 500 years of colonialism and IMF rule.

About two weeks ago, a truly historic conference, the International Conference on Lake Chad, took place in Abuja, Nigeria, where the historic Transaqua project was agreed upon by all the participating countries of the Lake Chad region. Transaqua is a monumental project. It involves taking 3 to 4% of the water from the tributaries of the Congo River, from an elevation of 500 meters, and flowing this water north through a canal system into Lake Chad. This is a transformational breakthrough, because not only will the currently dying Lake Chad be refilled and saved, but the project will create an inland shipping channel between the Democratic Republic of the Congo and Lake Chad, traversing all participating countries. The system will provide huge amounts of water for irrigation, and hydropower for the increasing electricity requirements of this growing region.

At that conference, an agreement was reached for a joint feasibility study between PowerChina, the large Chinese construction firm which built the Three Gorges Dam, and Bonifica, the Italian engineering firm that developed the Transaqua concept more than 30 years ago. At the same time, there was an agreement between China, Italy, and the participating African countries, that the Transaqua project is the only way that Lake Chad can be saved, and that only an inter-basin water transfer from the Congo Basin to the Lake Chad Basin, will solve the problem. They called on the African Union to support it, and thus extend development and also security throughout the entire Lake Chad region. They called on the African Development Bank to create a $50 billion fund for this project, to finance the canals, reforestation, and agriculture.

This is not an option, the governments at the conference said, but an absolutely urgent necessity. Over the past 60 years, Lake Chad has decreased in area by 95%, because of an extended drought with reduced rainfall, so that the surface area of the lake has shrunk from 26,000 sq. km in 1963, to less than 1,500 sq. km today. It's an ecological disaster. This has destroyed the livelihood of the people living there, and absent such an intervention, it will unquestionably cause a humanitarian crisis of unprecedented dimensions. It would extend the desertification of Africa.

This is the heart of Africa: The Lake Chad Basin is 8% of the total size of Africa. Eight countries are located there: Algeria, Cameroon, the Central African Republic, Chad, Libya, Niger, Nigeria, and Sudan. In these eight countries live 374 million people, 12% of them immediately around Lake Chad.

This is what Cheikh Anta Diop used to call "the cultural unity of Africa," and it was completely shattered with the 95% reduction of lake's area, leading to a total economic collapse. There was mass migration of people; nomads had to move their herds to try to find remaining pastureland. This also led to the rise of the Boko Haram terrorist organization.

The situation has reached such a total crisis point, that Nigerian President Muhammadu Buhari said at this conference that it is urgent to save Lake Chad, and there can be absolutely no delay.

Schiller Institute

The February 2018 Lake Chad conference.

He said, "The time to act is now, the time to bail out our region is now. The time to show our humanity is now."

There were many very skilled Nigerian water engineers at this conference, scientists who have been discussing this project for many decades. And there was a big debate, which I think is also very relevant, between UNESCO, on the one side, which said that water is a commodity with a price, as opposed to those who argued that water is a basic human right and that everyone must have sufficient safe, physically accessible, potable water, for consumption, cooking, and personal and domestic hygiene requirements.

A Transformed World

So Transaqua will lead to an industrial revolution in the heart of Africa. It will completely redefine the curriculum for African students, because literally millions of scientists, engineers, and experts must be educated and trained. And it will spin off many follow-on projects, leading to a broad industrialization of all of Africa.

PowerChina's lead engineer declared that, because the Italian government is providing 1.8 million euros for the feasibility study, it will be completed in only one year. An engineering feasibility study will be completed within the second year, and this engineer was confident that the entire project can be completed in twelve years. This is incredible, and further, with it will come a comprehensive system of highways and railways—all part of the extension of the New Silk Road, or the Belt and Road Initiative, into Africa.

Transaqua, upon which the relevant governments agreed as the only alternative, is also a beautiful model for cooperation among (a) China, along with (b) a European country, namely Italy, and (c) the African nations. And that, I think, is absolutely beautiful, because it also constitutes a breakthrough towards the similarly needed cooperation among Asian and Latin America nations, by demonstrating how countries from completely different cultural backgrounds can cooperate in such a beautiful project.

It is projected—I don't know if it's completely scientifically backed up—but it is projected that by 2050, the average temperatures in this Central African region will rise by 2 to 3 degrees. In that case, the drying up of Lake Chad would cease being a regional or even a Pan-African matter, becoming rather a global concern. From this standpoint, Transaqua is not an "option," but a necessity. Without it there will be an unbelievable humanitarian crisis. By the year 2040, there will be no fewer than two billion Africans, among them many, many young people who need jobs, who need education, and who need a positive hope for the future. But now, with Transaqua, I think Africa is on a good trajectory.

Lessons can be drawn for the Latin American situation, because here as well, the One Belt, One Road initiative expresses the true self-interest of Latin America. At the China-Community of Latin American and Caribbean States Forum in Chile on January 22, Chinese Foreign Minister Wang Yi offered the total cooperation of China in the development of the Latin American continent. Juan Carlos Varela, the President of Panama, who recently returned from a very important tour in China, said that with the help of China, there will soon be a high-speed rail line from Panama City to Chiriqui on the Costa Rican border. Soon after, it will connect all of Central America, and soon after that, all of the Americas.

Within a short period, then, there will be high-speed rail systems running from the southern tip of Argentina and Chile, crossing the Darien Gap, and going up all the way across the Bering Strait, thus connecting a great and unified transportation system of the Americas with the Eurasian corridors.

The geopolitical opposition in the United States, is of course opposed to that—but is the opposition surmountable? Well, President Varela, who wants cooperation with China, has also asked the United States to be part of it! The good thing is that President Trump has excellent relations with China's President Xi, the sort of President-to-President relationship which can really outflank the geopolitical opposition. Fifty-three percent of U.S. citizens are positive about China, despite the non-stop attacks by the mainstream media and the think-tanks. The United States itself has a huge infrastructure crisis: It doesn't have a high-speed rail system, as China does. Its aging infrastructure is rapidly rotting away. We have just witnessed the collapse of a brand new pedestrian bridge in Florida, killing six people, before it was even completed. Even its new infrastructure doesn't work!

Chinese experts estimate that the United States needs $8 trillion of investment in infrastructure to remedy its situation. China has $1.4 trillion of reserves in U.S. Treasuries, which could be invested in U.S. infrastructure through an infrastructure bank. It's clear that the neo-cons in the Republican Party do not want to provide budget resources for this investment, but Chinese-U.S. cooperation could lead to a solution of this problem, based on the major-power relationship concept proposed by Xi Jinping.

Will it be easy? Well, in light of what I said in the beginning about the geopolitical confrontation, as demonstrated by Theresa May—absolutely not! Therefore, what is needed is a mass movement for development. In Latin America we need hundreds of thousands and even millions, both young and old, demanding not only cooperation with China and the New Silk Road, but that the United States join in, seeing China and the Belt and Road projects not as a threat, but as a great opportunity for joint ventures.

Therefore, I appeal to all of you to create such a mass movement for development. There are also many Hispanic people in the United States, who need productive jobs, and a future. They can and must be part of this.

Begin a broad discussion around you about a vision: Where should the Americas be in 50 or 100 years? If China can eliminate all poverty among its citizens by 2020, why can't the Americas do that, too? Maybe we need five years. Maybe we need seven years, but not much more.

Rather than calling Chinese investment in Latin American "aggressive," as the head of the U.S. Southern Command, Adm. Kurt Tidd said, the United States, China, and Latin American countries should be cooperating in development projects, as we see now among China, Italy, and the African countries.

Mankind is different from all other species, in that we are human! We are not wolves, each of us set against all the other wolves. The economy is not a zero-sum game. As a human species, we can unite on a higher level of reason and be guided by a tremendous love for mankind! We can have a beautiful vision for the future of all of humanity. We are on the verge of making so many scientific breakthroughs. For example, China is very close to accomplishing thermonuclear fusion energy, and once we have that, we have not only energy security, but raw materials security as well. We can have nuclear-powered space flight, which will completely change the nature of space exploration. Soon we can build villages on the Moon, which can become the basis for further exploration of space. And in one generation, maybe two at most, we can have inter-stellar space travel, to explore the secrets of our galaxy, and maybe beyond.

When the New Silk Road becomes the World Land-Bridge, which is the program of the Schiller Institute, we will gain the material conditions for every child on this planet to have a universal education. The number of people who become geniuses will increase incredibly, and we will relate to each other in a truly human fashion, by relating to the creativity of the other person, rather than regarding him or her as a threat or a nuisance.

We are at a very exciting time in history. I personally think that the beautiful vision of Xi Jinping of completely transforming the world by 2050, so that everyone on this planet can have a happy life and a beautiful world, is definitely realizable. So, please, create a mass movement for development. That's the best thing you can do to accomplish that goal.

hz.zepp@schiller-institute.de

Apollo Mission on Earth: Transforming Our Relationship to the Physical World

by Bill Roberts

Bill Roberts reports from Michigan.

March 26—In the context of LaRouche PAC's "2018 Campaign to Win the Future," representatives of local and state governments, political campaign organizations, state level professional associations, and labor organizations have been in dialogue with associates of Lyndon LaRouche regarding the implementation of LaRouche's Four Economic Laws.

In the course of these discussions, driven largely by the need to find sources of funding for major infrastructure repairs and upgrades, important policy questions have emerged which reflect the need for a more in-depth visualization of what the next fifty to one hundred years of mankind will look like.

These questions include (1) Why cannot user fees capture all of the value in a system of National Banking? (2) Why is capital budgeting, rather than an annual appropriation of funds, required? (3) How do we determine the real, i.e., non-monetary, value of infrastructure? and (4) What will a more productive American work force and economy look like?

While I will not attempt to answer all of these questions right now, I would like to take a look at factors that will help answer the third question, factors that also relate to the other three questions.

After decades of living in a national economy lacking any real long-term goals or a science-driver mission, concepts such as the difference between economic value and financial value is not very well understood by infrastructure specialists or policymakers, let alone most professional economists.

If we are only working on finding ways to fund the maintenance of currently existing roads, bridges, dams, water and sewerage facilities, airports, and electrical grids, then securing Federal funding for infrastructure above the level of $1 to 2 trillion seems like a godsend. But in reality, such an approach is not adequate to secure a future in the way that China is currently demonstrating through its national economic planning. In order to understand why, we must start from the standpoint of human history and reality, not money.

Promethean Fire

Scientific revolutions create economic value by transforming man's relationship to the physical universe, and increase our productivity per capita as a spinoff. The level of energy-flux density utilized by man changes the way we are able to produce and use the various elements of the periodic table. Our ability to mass-produce aluminum, for example, depends upon the ability to produce a lot of electricity, cheaply. For identical reasons, it is not accidental that breakthroughs both in the mass production of chemical fertilizer and in the development of the atomic bomb, occurred within a short distance from the cheap and abundant electricity produced by the hydroelectric generation capacity built by the Tennessee Valley Authority.

In contrast, today, some energy providers will actually send specialists out to your residence, completely free of charge, to replace light bulbs and find other ways of minimizing electricity use, due to the advanced age and deteriorating condition of our power plants and electrical grids, and the lack of new generating capacity. Not only is increased energy capacity **not** being considered from the standpoint of what we could do qualitatively if we had more energy—but we are actually planning ahead for failure, for decreased energy generation capacity per capita.

Interregional City Clusters

Infrastructure upgrades (as with other capital investments)—the expansion of the infrastructure qualitatively and quantitatively—are necessitated not by the linear projection of current user habits, but by non-linear changes in mankind's behavior.

For example, over half of the trips on the busiest lines generated by the construction of China's 22,000 km of high-speed rail, are trips that would not occur if it were not for the availability of high-speed trains. Every year during the 40-day Spring Festival, there is a mass migration of roughly 385 million people travelling across the country and back, to vacation or visit family. If, instead, all of these people had cars, it would not be possible for them all to be on the road during this period. A certain proportion of the estimated 2.98 billion trips for *all* purposes during the 40 days, is what are called "generated trips," that is, trips produced as a function of social and economic attributes of households. The extent of construction of China's high-speed rail system is changing the social characteristics of the Chinese population.

Part of China's current economic vision is the development of city-clusters as integrated economic areas. China's National Development and Reform Commission has designated certain clusters of cities, such as those in the Beijing-Tianjin-Hebei (Jing-Jin-Ji) region, as interregional city clusters. Rather than building more rings of highways to expand megacities such as Beijing, which grow much faster than other cities, the plan is to have a larger area connected by fast, modern transportation, so that someone living anywhere in that region can commute to work anywhere else in the region within one hour.

Clusters of very large cities can thus function in the way that individual metro areas do now, with the added benefit that the labor market for any individual employer or city center is now larger—as large as 50 million people. One of the advantages is the option to concentrate, within each city of the cluster, a particular economic specialization, whether it be administration, manufacturing, technological development, or something else. A family does not have to choose between living where one spouse's dream job is, versus another opportunity, but can commute within an hour's time to any of multiple cities. As a result, more of the population can be employed in such a way as to maximize their productivity. It may well be the case that a certain number of these trips do not financially pay for themselves—yet!

But, from the standpoint of the division of labor required in a more advanced and more productive economy, such as an economic platform characterized by commercially available fusion power, such an arrangement is indispensable. To move society forward, capital investment of this sort is required.

Hypothetically, on a train capable of travelling at speeds of 230 mph, a commuter could travel from Detroit, Michigan to Cleveland, Ohio (170 miles) in about 45 minutes. Such a concept of integrating a mega-region with high-speed trains travelling at 230 mph, connecting multiple city centers to achieve economic regions of higher productivity per capita, should be considered for the Northeast Corridor, the Great Lakes Region, the Texas Triangle, and the West Coast.

In contrast, many East and West Coast U.S. cities currently suffer from massively overpriced real estate markets, requiring low-wage earners to live far outside their city centers and commute long distances in dense automobile traffic, to work in dead-end, non-productive jobs. Workers commute to Washington, D.C. from as far away as West Virginia—at least a 90-minute drive each way.

Henry Ford and the American System

An earlier example of how capital expenditures were necessitated by an intention to transform man's relationship to the physical world in a non-linear way, is the case of the Ford Motor Company in its early years. In 1914, when Henry Ford announced a pay raise from $2 a day to $5 a day for his employees, he actually saw it as a cost-*saving* measure, which in fact it turned out to be—even more successfully than he had imagined. He was opposed by his directors, some of whom thought they could get him to give up the idea by ridiculing it! The news was so shocking, that it was probably the biggest international news item in history ever, at the time.

The key to increasing productivity was not simply paying his workers more, although that was part of it; the pay raise was possible *because* of their higher productivity. As Henry Ford's spokesman explained the effect after the fact, increasing the wage of his workers made it possible for them to afford the Model T. That created a ripple-effect of increased earnings throughout the country, which, in turn, made the Model T affordable to many others.

Increasing the number of people who could purchase the Model T by raising wage levels throughout the country, and simultaneously bringing down the cost of his cars, was necessary for one simple reason:

The really massive capital investments that had the biggest effect on cost reduction, required a dramatic growth in the number of cars produced in order to justify the investment. In other words, in order to make the ownership of the personal automobile possible for the average American, Henry Ford had to think on the scale of the U.S. economy as a whole, and transform it.

In addition to more than doubling their hourly wage, Ford also reduced their work day from 10 to 8 hours, a significant drop from the grueling 60-hour work week that was the standard in American manufacturing at that time.

China's approach to international investments is not entirely different. It approaches loans and investments in infrastructure not from the standpoint of always maximizing profits, but sometimes to create the conditions for raising the standard of living and productivity of other nations' populations.

That is why Henry Ford decided to build the massive River Rouge Complex seven years after his plant in Highland Park, Michigan, opened, which itself had been designed to mass-produce the Model T, the first factory in the world to assemble cars on a moving assembly line. Ultimately, to make a car as affordable as possible, he decided he had to control all the costs, beginning with raw-materials extraction, making it possible to introduce cost-saving innovations throughout the entire manufacturing process, and thus requiring a fully integrated manufacturing process. The Rouge was designed to build cars from scratch, bringing in the raw materials directly on barges on the Detroit River.

The 2,000-acre mega-complex was the most technologically advanced manufacturing plant the world had ever seen, employing 103,000 workers at its peak in 1924. In order get the raw materials in, and the cars out, the Ford Motor Company had to purchase a railroad and dredge the Rouge River along a three-mile stretch connecting to the Detroit River.

The early history of the Ford Motor Company is riddled with opposition to Ford's reinvestment decisions by stockholders such as the Dodge brothers, who sued him over his policy. They opposed his boldest plans—the Rouge, for example—to reinvest company profits in state-of-the-art improvements in plant and equipment. Ford eventually gave ultimate authority over expenditures to the production departments, which were tasked with finding ways to bring the cost of production down to the price at which Ford wanted the car to be sold.

Henry Ford's right hand man and closest collaborator over forty years, Charlie Sorensen, described in his book, *My Forty Years with Ford*, how completely revolutionary and anti-British this approach was:

Until then, American business had operated on the principle that prices should be kept at the highest point at which people would buy. That is still the operating principle of much French and British industry. But the foundation of the American industrial system, which today out produces the world, is the mass production technique worked out at Ford Motor Company coupled with Henry Ford's economic heresies that higher wages and lower prices resulted in more abundant production at lower cost.

Like China's leadership today, Sorensen thought it better to tear down an old factory and build an entirely new one, rather than stick with old habits and old ideas, which, while profitable in the short term, ensured stagnation and eventual failure. Sorensen described his line of thinking in starting from scratch and building a new iron-smelting plant:

The need for such a superplant was stressed by our experience at Highland Park, which was based on the best we knew how, but also on the same practices that would have been familiar to Egyptian bronze casters of 2500 BC. When something new and different is sought, it is useless to copy; start fresh on a new idea. This means fresh minds at work. Seeking help on planning this new foundry, I had to cast aside all precedent, for there were no engineering groups that could or would satisfy our demands for something different.

Where there is no vision, the people perish.

Like the spirit of the New Silk Road, and like the Americans who understood where real value in an economy comes from, we too must endeavor to cast aside all precedent and craft a vision of the future—not from old habits and tricks, but rather by a total vision for the future, a mission orientation, like the Apollo mission, and then figure out how to make it possible.

bill.roberts.michigan@gmail.com

Martin Luther King's American Presidency

by Dennis Speed

Since prior to Plato, the fundamental issue of law within globally extended European civilization, has continued to be the conflict between two axiomatically irreconcilable notions of law and government, between the Classical standpoint of natural law, as typified by Plato and the Christianity of the New Testament, and that opposing, pagan tradition known today as the Romantic school of law, whose precedents included the customs of ancient Babylon and the Delphi cult of the Pythian Apollo.

It is only from that standpoint respecting law, that the phenomena of racism in modern society can be competently diagnosed.

—Lyndon LaRouche,
"The Tragedy of Education:
Shrunken Heads in America
Today."

Martin Luther King, Jr.

March 27—Often, probably always, it is better to ask an intelligent question, than to provide an inadequate or misleading answer, no matter how desirable or expedient that might be. So it is with almost every important process in current history. "Events" do not exist in themselves. There is, for example, no event termed "the Martin Luther King assassination" that is separate from "the Robert Kennedy assassination," and neither of those two "events" is comprehensible without understanding the assassination of President John F. Kennedy on November 22, 1963.

All three assassinations are one process, one "arc," itself part of a longer-term assault on the United States Presidency

President John F. Kennedy.

LBJ Library/Yoichi R. Okamoto
Robert F. Kennedy, Jan. 28, 1964.

Alexander Gardiner portrait
President Abraham Lincoln.

from its historical enemy: the assassination-bureaus of British intelligence. The British kill American Presidents, as they killed Abraham Lincoln. *EIR* has published much on this matter in the past, and it is not necessary to review that material here. The latest British attack on United States, the 2015-2018 assault on the Trump Presidential candidacy and Presidency, is, in method, identical to the British assault on the Presidency of 1994-1999, called "the impeachment of Bill Clinton." Today, the case officer is "former" MI6 agent Christopher Steele (and implicitly, "former" MI6 head Sir Richard Dearlove, of "Iraq has weapons of mass destruction" fame); then, the campaign's British intelligence operative was named Ambrose Evans-Pritchard. Whether Republican or Democrat, the American Presidential system, and the American system of self-government in particular, is the mortal enemy of the City of London—whether the American people are aware of that, or not.

The Presidential system devised by Alexander Hamilton and George Washington, especially as expressed in Hamilton's four great documents on manufactures, credit, the National Bank and the Constitutional basis for a National Bank, is anti-colonial, anti-imperial, and anti-Malthusian—that is , the "genetic opposite" of the predatory monetary culture which is London, at least from the global hegemony of the British East India Company, secured at the Treaty of Paris in 1763. East India Company apologists Thomas Malthus, John Locke, Adam Smith, David Hume, and precursors such as Thomas Hobbes, are not the philosophical founders of the American Revolution, but its mortal enemies. In Lyndon LaRouche's essay, "The Tragedy of Education: Shrunken Heads In America Today," he contends:

I say again, for emphasis, that the tradition of slaveholder interest, as defined by John Locke

oil portrait by Daniel Huntington, 1865
Alexander Hamilton

and his followers, has a vigorous reincarnation as the Locke doctrine of "shareholder interest" today. On today's global scale, that Locke doctrine, deployed under the name of "shareholder interest," has become as murderous and savage a pro-racist killer, as the old Locke doctrine of "slaveholder value" took pride in being. I shall not, and need not repeat here what is documented sufficiently elsewhere, on the relevant subject of the legacies of Jeremy Bentham's Aaron Burr and Burr's Martin van Buren, as by Anton Chaitkin's *Treason in America*.

Treasury Secretary Alexander Hamilton's economic revolution, documented in his four reports on Manufactures, the National Bank, Public Credit, and the Constitutionality of the National Bank, as expressed by his and George Washington's Presidency, are the only true basis for the eradication of slavery, racism, poverty and war. That economic revolution has been adopted, albeit with Chinese and Russian characteristics, by the presidencies of Xi Jinping and Vladimir Putin. Lyndon LaRouche's Four Laws are a singular principle, expressed in the sovereign power of the free citizens of, not only the United States, but each nation, to promote the creativity of the human mind as the primary source of wealth in a free nation. That can be the only true meaning of the term, the American System, when used in opposition to the British Imperial System of monetarism.

Martin Luther King's and Robert Kennedy's assassinations over the two-month period of April 4 through June 6, 1968, ultimately drowned the United States into a cultural pessimism from which it has yet to recover. That cultural weakness can now be summarily removed from American life, and in short order. All that is needed is the courage to do what Martin Luther King did: stand on the mountaintop of history.

Immortality

Like Lincoln, King gave two speeches that transformed American history. One was given under nearly optimal circumstances, "the best of times," on August 28, 1963. The other was given in "the worst of times," on April 3, 1968. The second is actually almost unknown, although many think they know it. They know the speech's end,—"I've been to the mountaintop!... Mine eyes have seen the glory of the coming of the Lord!"—but the speech's end cannot be understood without the beginning.

Between his April 4, 1967 Riverside Church speech opposing the war in Vietnam, and his April 4, 1968 assassination, King was nearly completely ostracized from liberal-Democratic America, except among those supporting Presidential candidate Eugene McCarthy. Polls asserted that 75 percent of America opposed his new direction. His fund-raising, infiltrated at the top of his organization, the Southern Christian Leadership Conference, by FBI informants capable of affecting policy, not only collapsed; the collapse was blamed on his stand on the Vietnam war, and his insistence on continuing his highly controversial "non-civil rights" Poor People's Campaign. King's move to support the sanitation workers of Memphis, Tennessee, was also precisely the opposite of what almost all of his closest staff, and closest collaborators supported. King was the object of assassination threats, and had just experienced a bomb scare on the plane that flew him to Memphis. King had been termed "out of date" by those in the Black Power movement, and by most college youth, even many of those in the anti-war movement.

The exhausted King had not wanted to give the speech at the Masonic Hall that evening, but his closest friend, Ralph Abernathy, whom he had sent in his stead, insisted. When he arrived, after saying a few words about his friend Ralph, King began:

As you know, if I were standing at the beginning of time, with the possibility of general and panoramic view of the whole human history up to

U.S. Library of Congress/Dick DeMarsico
Martin Luther King, Jr.

now, and the Almighty said to me, "Martin Luther King, which age would you like to live in?"—I would take my mental flight by Egypt through, or rather across the Red Sea, through the wilderness on toward the promised land. And in spite of its magnificence, I wouldn't stop there. I would move on by Greece, and take my mind to Mount Olympus. And I would see Plato, Aristotle, Socrates, Euripides and Aristophanes assembled around the Parthenon as they discussed the great and eternal issues of reality.

But I wouldn't stop there. I would go on, even to the great heyday of the Roman Empire. And I would see developments around there, through various emperors and leaders. But I wouldn't stop there. I would even come up to the day of the Renaissance, and get a quick picture of all that the Renaissance did for the cultural and esthetic life of man. But I wouldn't stop there. I would even go by the way that the man for whom I'm named had his habitat. And I would watch Martin Luther as he tacked his ninety-five theses on the door at the church in Wittenberg.

But I wouldn't stop there. I would come on up even to 1863, and watch a vacillating president by the name of Abraham Lincoln finally come to the conclusion that he had to sign the Emancipation Proclamation. But I wouldn't stop there. I would even come up to the early thirties, and see a man grappling with the problems of the bankruptcy of his nation. And come with an eloquent cry that we have nothing to fear but fear itself.

But I wouldn't stop there. Strangely enough, I would turn to the Almighty, and say, "If you allow me to live just a few years in the second half of the twentieth century, I will be happy." Now that's a strange statement to make, because the world is all messed up. The nation is sick. Trouble is in the land. Confusion all around. That's a strange statement. But I know, somehow, that only when it is dark enough, can you see the stars. And I see God working in this period of the twentieth century in a way that men, in some strange way, are responding—something is happening in our world. The masses of people are rising up. And wherever they are assembled today, whether they are in Johannesburg, South Africa; Nairobi, Kenya; Accra, Ghana; New York City; Atlanta, Georgia; Jackson, Mississippi; or Memphis, Tennessee—the cry is always the same—"We want to be free."

portrait by Joseph Siffred Duplessis, 1785
Benjamin Franklin

Gouverneur Morris

And another reason that I'm happy to live in this period is that we have been forced to a point where we're going to have to grapple with the problems that men have been trying to grapple with through history, but the demand didn't force them to do it. Survival demands that we grapple with them. Men, for years now, have been talking about war and peace. But now, no longer can they just talk about it. It is no longer a choice between violence and nonviolence in this world; it's nonviolence or nonexistence.

That view of immortality, and nothing else, is the true reason that Martin Luther King was marked for assassination. It was not the King that enjoyed triumph, but the King that "studied adversity" which expresses the greatest period in the life of Martin Luther King—that final year. The capacity of mind and soul to step outside of the cacophony of one's time, to point mankind, not merely a part of it, toward its higher purpose, is what the assassins of Martin Luther King hated. There was no way to remove King from the mountaintop. His qualification for the Presidency was his choice to live in immortality, rather than to live afraid. (See the video: "The Immortal Talent of Dr. King," of Lyndon LaRouche speaking to the MLK Prayer Breakfast of the Talladega County (Alabama) Democratic Conference, January 19, 2014.

Humanity and Inhumanity

The promotion, through "reputable" British and British-dominated educational institutions, of the myth that slave trader and Royal Africa Company founder John Locke was "the ideological father of the American Declaration of Independence and Constitution," rather than Benjamin Franklin, Alexander Hamilton, and the Constitution's *Preamble*'s author, Gouverneur Morris, is used to prevent Americans from understanding that the true intellectual leadership of the American Revolution was for the complete destruction of slavery. The three men cited were the precise moral opposite of John Locke. Franklin was the head of the Pennsylvania Anti-Slavery Society, Hamilton successfully organized for an African-American troop presence in the revolution, and Morris proposed the abolition of slavery to the 1787 Constitutional Convention. Their espoused notion of economics was opposite to that of Locke as well. The new United States had to be brought "up from slavery," however, to that higher idea of mankind.

The principles underlying the conceptions of economy and law that prevailed in the 1787-89 battle to establish a unified federal government, sovereign over any and all of the states, were later forcefully and nearly perfectly personified by Abraham Lincoln. Lincoln's personal evolution in the course of his 1861-1865 Presidency, particularly expressed in his relationship with the extraordinary Frederick Douglass, was inseparable from the evolution of the United States itself. And Lincoln's creation of the Transcontinental Railroad, in the course of his collaboration with Czar Alexander II of Russia, and even a still-British-colonized China, against the British and French-sponsored Confederacy, is an American gift to those nations that have now returned it in the form of the World Land-

Bridge policy proposed today to the United States by China's President Xi Jinping.

Martin Luther King's 1967-68 evolution was similar to that of Abraham Lincoln. King insisted, despite all warnings and all consequences, that he would assume responsibility for the nation as a whole, in order to change the nation in any part. He believed that "racism, poverty and war," all stemmed from one source: man's inhumanity to man. He knew, because he had already proven it, that holding political office was not a prerequisite to exercising the Constitutional powers guaranteed to all American citizens. Economic justice, he believed, was an inalienable right. Creative nonviolent direct action was his chosen way to incorporate increasingly larger numbers of people, who believed themselves to be powerless, into a living, comprehensive, continuous Constitutional Convention distinguished by improvement through changing the axioms of social practice of a far-less-than-perfect United States.

National Park Service

Martin Luther King, Jr., addressing a crowd from the steps of the Lincoln Memorial, where he delivered his "I have a dream" speech during the Aug. 28, 1963 march on Washington, D.C.

Let The Trumpet Sound

That "more perfect Union," the United States of the future, was precisely that to which Martin Luther King spoke on August 28, 1963. The speech he gave that day, at least in part, was intended by King as a speech to be delivered by President John Kennedy on January 1, 1963's 100th anniversary of the Emancipation Proclamation. Kennedy, however, declined. It was called "the American Dream." King spoke about it several times that year, including in an appearance in Detroit's Cobo Hall before an estimated 25,000 people. In Washington, however, in the shadow of Daniel Chester French's seated Lincoln, King added something. He did it at the instigation of singer Mahalia Jackson, who had noticed that the 250,000 people assembled, though moved, needed to be elevated past the present, to see the complex domain of the future in the present. This extraordinary gathering, the largest at that time in American history, was no longer about civil rights; it was about the nature and purpose of man, from whence are derived the inalienable rights expressed in the Declaration of Independence. "Behold, I tell you a mystery. We shall not die, but we shall all be changed... For the trumpet shall sound, and the dead shall be raised, incorruptible."

That is what Mahalia Jackson called upon Martin to do—not to preach, but to do: raise the dead. "Tell 'em about the dream, Martin!"

A Greek playwright, such as the young Aeschylus of 495 B.C.E., would have recognized what King actually did in that speech's conclusion immediately. He employed the principle of the Greek chorus. It was not Martin Luther King that now spoke, but the resurrected Lincoln, in the form of the actor Martin Luther King. Then, the Founders of the United States, the prophet Isaiah and the composer G.W.F. Handel were brought in rapid succession onto the stage now being created in the mind of the audience. Next, the audience involuntarily and silently sang, in their minds, "My Country, 'Tis of Thee," while King shifted from the refrain, "I have a dream," to the refrain "Let Freedom Ring." The Classical training in what is sometimes called elocution—not the same thing as rhetoric, with which it is sometimes confused—had never been witnessed by so many people of such diverse backgrounds at all, let alone from an African-American preacher not yet old enough to be President.

Clarence Jones, who had worked on a draft of the speech with King, recounted in an interview:

Mahalia Jackson, his favorite gospel singer, yells out to him, "Tell 'em about the dream, Martin! Tell 'em about the dream!" Now, I'm standing behind him, and I see what he does when he hears her shout back to him—he then takes the papers on the lectern, and he moves them to the left. And he grabs the lectern podium, and I turn to some unknown person, and I said to them: "These people don't know it, but they are getting ready to go to church!"

(Note: King had begun his speech as the voice of the Lincoln seated behind him: "Five score years ago, a great American in whose symbolic shadow we stand today, signed the Emancipation Proclamation." He had ended that speech as the voice of Frederick Douglass and the African-American Spiritual: "Free At Last.")

The Targeting of King

The head of the FBI's domestic intelligence division, William Sullivan, was not moved by the spirit. He wrote in a memo that the speech solidified King "as the most dangerous Negro of the future in this Nation from the standpoint of communism, the Negro and national security." President Kennedy, as author Taylor Branch recounts in *Parting The Waters: America In The King Years*, "was watching a complete King speech for the first time. 'He's damn good,' the President remarked to his aides at the White House. . . . As the principal leaders filed into the Cabinet Room from the march, he greeted King with a smiling 'I have a dream'. . ." J. Edgar Hoover, the informal but de facto successor to Albert Pike, the 19th Century judicial officer of the Ku Klux Klan, now escalated his already-existent surveillance and slander campaign against King.

Martin Luther King, from the time of the 1963 "March on Washington," was now a part of the American Presidential System. This became clearer with the passage of the 1964 Civil Rights Act and the 1965 Voting Rights Act. Such an inclusion, however, just as in the case of Lyndon LaRouche's inclusion in the Presidential System from the late 1970s, does not mean that one is

National Archives/George K. Warren

Frederick Douglass, ca. 1879.

necessarily accepted. In fact, it may signal the onset of vicious harassment, leading to financial ruination, destruction of family life, illegal arrest and physical assault. John Kennedy, Robert Kennedy, and Ronald Reagan were presidents or presidential aspirants who were shot. Why would private citizens operating on the principle of the General Welfare, but on the level of the Presidency, necessarily fare better, especially if they are effective?

Being included, in the case of King, meant taking a walk with President Kennedy outside of the Oval Office, about two months prior to the March on Washington.

In his book, *The FBI and Martin Luther King, Jr.*, David Garrow describes the meeting:

That afternoon, after a meeting of the assembled civil rights leadership with the president, John Kennedy himself took King out into the Rose Garden. Kennedy, according to an account that King later gave three close friends, asked King, "you've read about Profumo in the papers?" King had. Kennedy went on, "that was an example of friendship and loyalty carried too far. Macmillan is likely to lose his government because he has been loyal to his friend. You must take care not to lose your cause for the same reason." Kennedy then named Levison and O'Dell. [Stanley Levison and Jack O'Dell, two key allies of Martin

Stanley Levison, an ally of Martin Luther King in the Southern Christian Leadership Conference.

Luther King in the Southern Christian Leadership Conference.] "They are communists. You've got to get rid of them." He pointed out that public exposure of the Levison and O'Dell allegations would affect not only King but the entire civil rights effort and the administration's civil rights bill as well. "If they shoot you down, they'll shoot us down too—so we're asking you to be careful." The president went on to warn King that these opponents of civil rights would have him under very close surveillance. King should keep this in mind. King indicated that he appreciated that, and he did not quarrel with the president about O'Dell. But about Levison he felt differently. "I know Stanley," he told John Kennedy, "and I can't believe this. You will have to prove it." The president paused, and then said that he would arrange for Burke Marshall to give proof of the matter to King. With that the brief stroll and conversation ended.

King had found the experiences of that day both troubling and amusing. He joked to Andrew Young that the president must be worried about someone bugging him as well. Why else would he have taken King into the Rose Garden to talk? The conversations had not created doubt within him about Levison, or, for that matter, O'Dell. But King was troubled by the great consternation that the Kennedy brothers and Marshall were exhibiting. He made no move to sever ties with either or doubt Levison, however....

This past October, when some final portions of the up-to-now unclassified papers on the Kennedy assassination were released, a 27-page memo entitled "Martin Luther King Jr., A Current Analysis," was found contained in them. Some contended that this was some sort of filing error, until it was pointed out that the FBI memo, dated March 12, 1968, a mere three weeks before King's assassination, had been re-classified on May 8, 1994! That is, it had been read, or at least reviewed, and had been re-classified, and not even under

U.S. Library of Congress

Demonstrators participating in the Poor People's March in Washington, D.C., 1968.

King's name, but under JFK. Nothing in the memo's contents links King to any "business" with Kennedy whatsoever. What it does make clear, is how dangerous the upcoming Poor People's campaign was seen to be by the FBI. One section of the memo states:

> King has referred to this campaign as the "Washington spring project" and the "poor peoples march," which is reportedly being staged to pressure Congress into passing legislation favorable to the Negro. It is King's contention that the government of the United States does not move until it is confronted dramatically. To add to the dramatic confrontation, King has boasted he and his entourage are coming to Washington to stay; that his followers will conduct sit-ins, camp-ins, and sleep-ins at every government facility available including the lawn of the White House. He has bragged that he will fill up the jails of Washington and surrounding towns....

The Real Presidential Assassins

While there is no question that the FBI's role was nefarious, it was because of King's evolution after the Nobel Peace Prize was awarded to him in 1964, and after the successful Selma Campaign of 1965, that he became marked for death. Samuel P. Huntington, of "Clash of Civilizations" notoriety, argued in his book, *The Crisis of Democracy,* that there must remain a

"Chinese Wall" between the functions of "electoral advocacy" and "governance" to allow modern society to be "orderly." Governing had now to be left to an elite managerial class of reliable civil servants, British style. Anyone could be allowed to advocate whatever they wished, and limited change within policy-making circles in governments could be tolerated or even encouraged. Under no circumstances, however, should common citizens, or even uncommon citizens, be allowed to bring the powerless into the corridors of power, except as tourists. If one allowed that, then "democracy" would undergo the

McGeorge Bundy, Special Assistant to President Kennedy for National Security.

crisis that the bureaucracy that perpetually actually rules, would no longer be allowed to do so. Nothing would get done, because accountability would be demanded. King's threat to combine the common self-interest of poor whites, poor African-Americans, poor Mexicans and immigrants, with those of students, trade unionists and others, would pose that risk. His movement had succeeded in forcing through the 1965 Voting Rights Act, which dissolved the Southern segregationist Democratic Party, actively in power since 1876. What would happen if, now, he turned his attention to international questions, like the war in Vietnam, or the elimination of poverty worldwide? What would become of the neo-Malthusian agenda to which British imperial policy was devoted?

The King movement had to be disrupted from the inside—both inside the African-American community, and inside his own organization. It had to be handled as ruthlessly as the way that the State Department was trying to handle the people of Vietnam— "Vietnamization." McGeorge Bundy, sometimes referred to as the acting head of the Anglo-American Establishment, deployed away from the National Security Council, where he had prosecuted and escalated the Johnson Administration's war on Vietnam, to become the president of the Ford Foundation, then the largest foundation in the United States. He took charge of what was referred to as the "Black Power project," once he assumed leadership of the Ford Foundation in the Summer of 1966. In an Aug. 2, 1966 speech in Philadelphia to the National Urban League, Bundy said, "We believe that equality for all American Negroes is now the most urgent domestic concern of this country. We believe that the Ford Foundation must play its part in this field because it is dedicated by its charter to human welfare." What Bundy was in fact after, was the dismantling of King's movement, utilizing "radical black nationalism" as a battering ram against it, while also buying off the debt-strapped SCLC.

In his work, *Black Awakening in Capitalist America*, Robert L. Allen put it this way:

From his years in working in the U.S. power structure, Bundy had nurtured a keen appreciation for the complexities involved in political manipulation and the seemingly contradictory policies which often must be pursued simultaneously in order to obtain a given end. Bundy learned that it is necessary to work both sides of the street… Hence he was a strong supporter of Kennedy's and Johnson's war policies in Vietnam, while at the same time stressing the necessity of keeping channels open to the Soviet Union. Such a man was perfectly suited to work with black groups, including black power advocates, while at the same time local governments were arming and preparing to use force to suppress the black communities. The seeming contradiction here, to use Bundy's word, was only a "surface" manifestation.

Bundy recruited two contacts recommended to him either directly by King or his close associates. These persons then influenced the SCLC and King, including by writing a "report on poverty" that King delivered as SCLC's own at a United States Senate hearing. A nervous Stanley Levison said to Andrew Young, "I don't want

Stokely Carmichael, former associate of Martin Luther King, speaking in London, 1990.

five million dollars. I want less. Five million dollars could destroy us," not recognizing that taking any money from the Ford Foundation at all, was the problem.

Meanwhile, British Intelligence—generally deployed against the United States on the cultural flank through Aldous Huxley's 30-plus year presence in California, and the promotion of various forms of "the British Invasion" in culture—studied "the African-American Black Power specimen" in London, in the course of two weeks (July 15-30, 1967), at something called "To Free A Generation: The Dialectics of Liberation Conference." Stokely Carmichael, formerly associated with King through his involvement in the Alabama Voting Rights Project, and the primary figure selected by the American media as "the voice of Black Power" replacing the *passé* Dr. King, attended. Carmichael was selected as the center of attention by Gregory Bateson, Margaret Meade, R.D. Laing, D.G. Cooper, and Herbert Marcuse—a Tavistock Institute/Frankfurt School "Dream Team" of brainwashers, against whom only a Malcolm X could contend. They calmly, each in his or her peculiar way—allowing Stokely to speak often—analyzed the Black Power phenomenon, which the Ford Foundation had partially created, from their psycho-surgical vantage point, without wishing to alert or upset either the victim or his associates. (The same exercise had been done, and would again later be done, by American brainwasher Kenneth Clark and the same "Dame" Margaret Mead on the much tougher James Baldwin, in their search to make sure, if possible, that the "Malcolm X/Martin Luther King syndrome" would never occur again.)

King's April 4, 1967 denunciation of the predatory population war in Vietnam, and his additional rise above civil rights in the form of the Poor People's campaign—organized on behalf of all poor Americans, not merely African-Americans—derailed the Ford Foundation and the brainwashers completely. He refused to go "back in the Black box." Robert Kennedy's entry into the Presidential race, although belated, now meant that a Kennedy Presidency—a Kennedy Presidency implicitly backed by even a non-committed King in the form of his months-long Poor People's Campaign—would activate untold numbers of new voters. These voters came from families that had been kept away from the polls since at least the time of Franklin Roosevelt's Presidency, if indeed they had ever voted at all. That "crisis of democracy" could not be allowed. Both Kennedy and King had to die. The British, and their Anglo-American counterparts agreed: "We did it in November, 1963. We can do it again."

China, Russia, and other nations yearn to see the return of the United States that once produced Martin Luther King, and to collaborate with the America for which King gave his last full measure of devotion. Now, fifty years later, the American Presidency is again poised to be unleashed. Earth's next fifty years begins now. If this American Presidency is to lead this country to again adopt its original revolutionary, anti-colonial, sovereign self-governing system—the true system of the "American" Revolution—it will be the result of creative direct action taken by each committed American citizen on behalf of that objective. The Presidency must be free to function in the interest of the United States as a whole. The clean-out of the treasonous factions of British intelligence inside of the FBI and other agencies, and the energetic advocacy of the World Land-Bridge by those who love mankind, will help bend the arc of King's moral universe ever more sharply and quickly toward justice, sooner than we might have hoped—or dreamed.

Is This Finally the Time When the War on the British-Run Drug Traffic Can Be Won?

by Ernest Schapiro, MD

March 25—Today we are witnessing an acceleration of the march to complete victory in the British Opium War against the United States. Eight states have already legalized marijuana for recreational purposes, and Vermont and Washington, D.C. allow marijuana possession and growing. Now, the Governor of the agro-industrial state of New Jersey, Phil Murphy, for many years a top Goldman Sachs banker, and ambassador to Germany from

2009 to 2013, intends to legalize marijuana use, and the current debate in New Jersey is limited to the varying degrees of repeal of the marijuana laws—this despite the fact that, in federal law, marijuana is a Schedule I narcotic, which is defined as having a high addictive potential and no medical use.

One of the outcomes of the intended legislation will be prescription of marijuana to smoke for supposed medical purposes, and also the full availability of places to purchase marijuana for "recreational" use.

From the time in the late 1970s when I was a founder of the National Anti-Drug Coalition, our nation has been on a descent into Hell. Whereas at that time, marijuana used in the United States was mostly imported from South America, now it

Phil Murphy on legal marijuana: 2019 Budget Address

is grown domestically, especially in California, and it is by far the biggest cash crop there. Whereas there is speculation in the media concerning whether legalization will lead to an increase in use, the answer is obvious, particularly among young people. Over a forty-year period, their usage rates have varied by a range of close to 100%, and that rate has been strikingly inverse to perceived risk. Legalization tells the young person that it can't be dangerous after all. As I will address a little later, the history of the many centuries of widespread hashish consumption in Islamic countries such as Egypt and Morocco, shows a collapse of civilization and the apparent impossibility of eradicating the highly addictive and motivation-destroying drug.

The Enemy: Dope, Inc.

In 1977 and 1978 our organization, the Lyndon LaRouche movement, clearly perceived the danger, because we recognized the intent of the British in conducting an Opium War against our nation. This was the result of our unique intelligence capabilities, our international deployment as a single organization, and above all, Lyndon LaRouche's method of hypothesis. We published our

Headquarters of money laundering HSBC today (left) and its 1865 crest (right) from its Opium War roots, which incorporates the UK royal coat of arms.

findings in *Dope, Inc.*[1] By that time, we had recognized that there was a fundamental, implacable conflict between the British system of empire and the intention of the American republican tradition. We traced the history of the conflict between Britain and America and identified the key adversarial figures.

Through LaRouche's work in physical economy, we were alerted to anomalies in global financial flows and balances of payments. This led us to an investigation of the vast array of "offshore" financial institutions, the great majority in small places under the control of the British and Dutch crowns. One of the most notorious was the Hong Kong and Shanghai Bank, which just then was applying for a New York State charter allowing it to buy the Marine Midland Bank, the biggest bank in western New York state, which includes Buffalo, where I was living. A case of the useful role of our international deployment was in Canada: In our exposé of Edgar Bronfman, a key figure in Dope, Inc., we had a confrontation with Louis Mortimer Bloomfield, whose law firm represented Bronfman. When I saw the report, I told our leadership that Bloomfield was a key figure in the JFK assassination, based on a book, *The Kennedy Conspiracy,* by Paris Flammonde,[2] which I read in 1973, a year

before I joined LaRouche's movement. I believe that had we not written *Dope, Inc.,* no one else could have done what we did. It required a kind of creative non-inductive leap based on LaRouche's insistence on seeking universal principles. Furthermore, once we had discovered the ordering principle, we were able to fill in the picture, including the offshore banks and the actual role of organized crime, including the way it operates through secret ethnic societies. That included the Anti-Defamation League of B'nai B'rith and its protégés—Meyer Lansky, Edgar Bronfman, Max Fisher, and Mo Dalitz.

Armed with this book and our strategically distributed locations, both in North and South America and in western Europe, we were a tremendous threat early on. I was privileged to be a participant. Buffalo was a strategic location, as I said, because of the Marine Midland fight. I ran for school board and was able to make this a public issue. Marijuana had recently been decriminalized by the New York legislature at the behest of Governor Hugh Carey, and I was able to get up impromptu at a dinner of the Buffalo Teachers Federation, to which a member had invited me, and denounce it for supporting the legislation. I got the endorsement of several ministers, including the bishop of the Church of God in Christ, and the President of the National Council of Catholic Physicians, who lived in Buffalo. I spoke in many church services. The key organizing weapons were the *Dope, Inc.* book and our magazine, *War On Drugs*, for which we sold thousands of subscriptions on the street and in my case, over the phone, to local clergy and small businesses. Our

---

1. *Dope, Inc. Britain's Opium War against the U.S.,* by a U.S. Labor Party Investigating Team, New Benjamin Franklin Publishing House, New York, 1978. The book has gone through subsequent editions published by *EIR.* The latest, in 2010, is available at http://store.larouchepub.com/product-p/eirbk-2010-1-0-0-std.htm. It has also had a Spanish edition, *Narcotraffico, S.A.*

2. Paris Flammonde, The Kennedy Conspiracy: An Uncommissioned Report on the Jim Garrison Investigation (New York: Meredith Press, 1969).

meetings were large; in one case a church brought a bus-load of people.

The response we got from the enemy was very instructive. The power of what we were doing forced the enemy to crush the National Anti-Drug Coalition (NADC) we had helped organize. The *Chicago Sun Times* and Illinois Attorney General Tyrone Fahner had the NADC banned in Illinois in 1982.[3] Their assault on us featured the charge that we were anti-Semitic! Despite that, we won victories in the 1986 Illinois primaries. Janice Hart won the Democratic primary for Secretary of State, and Mark Fairchild won the primary for Lt. Governor. Judge Albert V. Bryan lied;[4] we were indeed a clear and present danger.

Legalization Has Been Tried Before

The power of Dope, Inc., to wag the tongues of the media, politicians, and corrupt health and other professionals is shown by the still-repeated story that marijuana is not harmful. I can elaborate the experience of the Islamic countries over many centuries, as reported by Dr. Gabriel Nahas[5] in print and in his 1974 Congressional testimony, and by Egyptian psychologist Dr. M.I. Soueif in his very extensive study of male prisoners.[6] The earlier high civilization of the Islamic world as a whole was destroyed, and a large portion of the male work-force debilitated. The Sufi cults encouraged its use, and the story is told that Hasan-i Sabbah, the Old

Lyndon LaRouche's National Anti-Drug Coalition and the first issue of its War on Drugs *magazine, June 1980.*

Man of the Mountain, ran a stable of political assassins who were so named from the word hashish.[7] It was noted in Islamic chronicles and poetry, as well as the writings of European travelers, that hashish users were not only unfit for any but the simplest tasks, but also that they often went on to opium, as also reported by Dr. Soueif.

One problem that was not known in the Islamic world was the effects of young women's usage in damaging the fetal brain. There is evidence that marijuana causes "miswiring" of nerve fibers in the fetal brain, because the receptor of the normal endocannabinoid system guides their connecting with one another, and its function is injured by marijuana.[8] The younger the user, through adolescence, the more developmental harm is suffered.[9]

Dr. Soueif stressed that the more intelligent the hashish addict had once been, the more loss of cognitive power he suffered. This becomes relevant to the fact that for a considerable period, the Islamic world was ahead of Europe in the quality of scientific discovery, astronomy, navigation, and medicine, and that this

---

3. Christian Curtis, "Anti-Drug Group Sues ADL and Sun-Times," *Executive Intelligence Review,* Volume 9 Number 14: 1982.

4. *Railroad,* Commission to Investigate Human Rights Violations, Washington D.C. 1989, page xxiv.

5. Gabriel Nahas, M.D., Ph.D., "Hashish in Islam, 9th to 18th Century," *Bulletin of the N.Y. Academy of Sciences*, Vol. 58 #9, Dec. 1982. Gabriel Nahas, M.D. Ph.D., *Keep Off the Grass* (Paul S. Eriksson Publisher: 1990, Fifth Edition).

6. *"Marijuana-Hashish Epidemic and Its Impact on United States Security*," Hearings by the Subcommittee to Investigate the Administration of the Internal Security Act and Other Internal Security Laws, Committee on the Judiciary, U.S. Senate, 1974. See https://archive.org/details/marihuanahashish00unit

7. The word assassin derives from Hasan-i Sabbah's political murder cult in the 11th and 12th Centuries. Members were called "Hashishin," meaning "hashish eaters."

8. G. Tortoriello, et al., "Miswiring the Brain," *EMBO Journal*, 2014 Vol 33 Number 7, 668-685.

9. Nora Volkow, et al., "Adverse Effects of Marijuana Use," *New England Journal of Medicine,* 2014, Volume 370, (23): 2219-2217.

cultural advantage and gift to mankind as a whole was destroyed by centuries of unchecked hashish use. This centuries-long history of the catastrophic effects of widespread cannabis use in the Islamic world has been well known to the British Empire's "Arabic" scholars at Oxford and Cambridge for decades. Yet, nothing is ever said about it in the American and European press, because if such knowledge became widespread, it would upset the plans of Dope, Inc. today. Uncovering, by astute historians, of the Dope, Inc. of that period would be of considerable value for us today.

What Marijuana Does to the Brain

It has been shown in new studies that marijuana is comparable in its effects on brain circuits and neurotransmitters to other addictive drugs[10] and that it is comparable to cocaine in addicting power, and as difficult to quit. It is especially dangerous for people with a tendency to schizophrenia.[11] It brings the full-blown disorder on at an earlier age and makes it much more severe. Siblings of schizophrenics are therefore advised not to touch it.[12] Marijuana destroys executive function,[13] i.e., the ability to make judgments, observe one's inner emotional state, make decisions, and delay gratification. It, in effect, destroys free will, leaving a compulsion to take the drug in increasing amounts as tolerance develops. In place of creative reason the victim engages in magical thinking and is more suggestible.[14] That is, it increases impulsivity—of obvious relevance to the "new violence." One never hears about whether today's mass killers have been using marijuana. Effectively, marijuana destroys the fac-

Dr. Gabriel Nahas, 1920-2012.

ulties which make us human; the ability of the creative faculties to govern the sensual or erotic is removed.[15]

Medical marijuana has always been a fraud. Marijuana contains dozens of compounds, including the chief intoxicant, tetrahydrocannabinol (THC). Many of these compounds have been isolated and tested. Some of them have potential benefits, especially cannabidiol, without the intoxicating effects of THC. Therefore, allowing people to become intoxicated and addicted by smoking marijuana on the pretext of medical benefit has no justification, since any medical benefits can be derived from the isolated components. Medical marijuana is a monstrous lie and a fraud.

It should be kept in mind that under federal law, marijuana is still classified as a Schedule I drug. That means it has no medical use, a high potential for abuse, and the potential to create severe psychological and/or physical dependence. Therefore, the President has the authority to declare null and void all of the state laws which contravene that scheduling. This highlights the fact that to this day, no one in the executive branch or the Congress has been willing to declare that Britain is leading an opium war against this nation. I believe this is due to a combination of fear—that they will be subjected to the same treatment we received—and to a lack of intellectual guts. A case of the latter was our close contact, Dr. Gabriel Nahas, who knew the role of the British through his extensive study of the history of the drug trade and the fight by the Chinese and the Islamic countries against the British for agreements to end the traffic in opiates and marijuana.

If we are successful in turning the British overplaying their hand, as in the Skripal affair, and their obvious effort to destroy President Trump's collaboration with China and Russia, into an understanding of their underlying malevolent intent, it should be possible for Americans to finally make the connection of the British to drugs. Then, but only then, will Dope, Inc. become a thing of the past, along with the rest of geopolitics.

10. Volkow, Nora, ibid.; Wrege, Johannes et al., "Effects of Cannabis on Impulsivity: A Systematic Review of Neuroimaging Findings," *Current Pharmaceutical Design*, April 2014, Vol. 20 number 13.

11. "Marijuana and Cannabinoids: A Neuroscience Research Summit," NIDA/NIH, March 22-23, 2016, Video. On March 22: First speaker is Dr. Eden Evans, "Adolescent Cannabis Use Increases Risk for Psychosis." She discusses relation to onset of schizophrenia. Second speaker, Dr. Alan Budney, "Adolescent Cannabis Phenomenology, Prevalence, Outcomes, and Problems." He discusses the comparative addictive power of marijuana and cocaine and aspects of addiction. See at https://www.youtube.com/watch?v=Gx5P_RXn6ds

12. See video, reference 11.

13. See references in 10.

14. Testimony of Dr. Andrew Malcolm, reference 6.

15. Lyndon LaRouche, "Remarks on Gurwitsch's Method, Part 2," *21st Century Science and Technology,* Fall 1998, pages 54-57. "These [the erotic and the agapic—ES] are two distinct kinds of morphogenetic development of the personality. As such, each must have its own peculiar physiological substrate."

ZEPP-LAROUCHE WEBCAST

Desperation Forces British Imperial Elites into a Major Blunder

This is the edited transcript of the March 22, 2018 Schiller Institute New Paradigm webcast, an interview with the founder of the Schiller Institutes, Helga Zepp-La-Rouche. She was interviewed by Harley Schlanger. A video *of the webcast is available.*

Harley Schlanger: Hello. I'm Harley Schlanger. Welcome to this week's Schiller Institute international webcast, featuring our founder Helga Zepp-LaRouche.

The British have been in an open assault against Russia and Russian President Putin, using the Skripal case as the basis for that, with British Prime Minister Theresa May going completely wild in trying to build a unified front against Russia, and implicitly, against President Trump's efforts to establish cooperative relationships between the United States and Russia. This was just completely outflanked by a phone discussion between President Trump and Vladimir Putin. So we have lots to cover today, but I'd like to start there, with the significance of the Trump-Putin discussion, Helga.

Helga Zepp-LaRouche: I think this was a brilliant outflanking of this British operation. Just as Russiagate had almost collapsed in the United States and had actually turned against the role of British intelligence in this whole thing, that was the moment when Theresa May launched her incredible provocation against Russia. This was a clear effort to push President Trump into a corner, hoping he would not dare to try to make good on his promise to improve relations with Russia.

President Trump, instead, congratulated Putin on his re-election for another six years, and discussed the

UK Prime Minister Theresa May.

very, very important global issues confronting the world: strategic stability, preventing an arms race, and the crises in Syria, Ukraine, and Korea. The two presidents once again reconfirmed an important direct connection. This makes clear that the British effort is nothing but an insane attempted provocation.

It's also very important that in that same phone call, President Trump not only congratulated Putin for his re-election, but he also was very positive about the fact that China had removed term limits on its presidency so President Xi Jinping will be able to stay on in these crucial years ahead. Trump said this is very good, because President Xi Jinping has provided very, very good leadership.

The geopolitical faction is going wild, which is reflected in hysterical media coverage. But *it is good* that there is a relationship and a dialogue among the presidents of the three most important countries on the planet—the United States, Russia, and China. Every-

NATO Secretary General Jens Stoltenberg.

German Chancellor Angela Merkel and French President François Macron.

one who loves peace and who is not a moron should be happy about those relationships. If you contrast that with the rather unbelievable warmongering of Jens Stoltenberg, the head of NATO—this guy basically said that the poison attack on Skripal, the former double agent, means there is a likelihood of Russia dropping nuclear bombs—this is really crazy.

The war faction has gone beyond all reason. German Chancellor Angela Merkel, EUthe accuser has to provide evidence, not the accused, and that is exactly what Russian Foreign Minister Lavrov said. He used that occasion to say that Merkel's behavior, unfortunately, demonstrates that the European leaders have not yet found their way back to reason.

I think nothing can be expected from the Europeans at this point. The British are on a rampage; Merkel and Macron, for their own reasons, backed this up completely. It is very good that President Trump cut through all this hysteria and directly contacted Putin. After that telephone discussion, President Trump announced that they will have a summit fairly soon between the two of them. Serbia offered Belgrade as a neutral place for Putin and Trump to meet. I think this is a very, very good sign.

Schlanger: There have been a number of other discussions that I think are quite significant between the United States and Russian military, political leaders, and a briefing at the Russian Foreign Minis-

U.S. Senator Rand Paul (R-Ky.).

try. It does appear that the Trump administration and the Putin administration see this as an opportunity for outflanking the British provocations. Is that your assessment?

Zepp-LaRouche: Yes. As you said, there were all kinds of other diplomatic initiatives. The two military chiefs of staff communicated. There was a meeting between Russian Ambassador Anatoly Antonov and Senator Rand Paul, which is very important, because in the midst of all of this demonization, almost nobody dared to speak with the Russian Ambassador—because of what happened to Sessions. Ambassador Antonov and Rand Paul agreed to re-establish the United States-Russian inter-parliamentary dialogue.

Every effort to re-establish dialogue and trust building, confidence building, is an extremely welcome change. There was a policy of rapprochement through cooperation, and détente between Eastern Europe and Western Europe in the 1960s and 70s, trying to have a good-neighbor relationship in Europe. The dangerous and provocative approach really began with PNAC, the Project for a New American Century, led by the neo-cons when the Soviet Union collapsed. That led to NATO expansion, regime change, and interventionist wars. This so poisoned the atmosphere that you must really ask: what was the purpose—or what *is* the purpose of that? Why are the British trying to build such a war-like enemy image of Russia? There are a few, lonely voices who share our view, that once you build up such an enemy image, and you poison the atmosphere by making completely wild accusations, you are creating the kind of atmosphere in which things can go **very quickly, very wrong**, and that would be devastating.

In this context, it's also noteworthy that there was a Senate Armed Services Committee hearing, where General John Hyten, Commander of the U.S. Strategic Command, was asked: Does the United States at this point have any defense against the kinds of weapons systems which were announced by President Putin on March 1? And he said, no. Hyten continued, saying that the use of low-yield nuclear weapons should be more strongly considered as put forward in the U.S. 2018 Nuclear Posture Review. He was immediately refuted by a Democratic Senator who said no one should think that the use of so-called "low-yield nuclear weapons" could not immediately lead to an all-out nuclear war.

People should not blindly repeat this Cold War demonization against Russia—which is in a certain sense also against China—because this is *really* dangerous. It's very dangerous. The present crop of politicians in leading positions, with the exception of President Trump and a few others, seem to have been so self-brainwashed, and are so incapable of strategic thinking, or even thinking of the consequences of what they're saying and doing, that they are not capable of seeing either the causes or the effects of their warmongering. We need serious discussion of this danger; we need cooperation, confidence-building, dialogue, cooperation on economic projects, and cooperation in space as positive steps forward. This kind of confrontation should stop. We should support President Trump when he is trying to mend fences with Russia and China, and not attack him.

Schlanger: There is a counterattack against May from within the United Kingdom, from Labour Party Leader Jeremy Corbyn, even from some of the people in the chemical weapons section of British intelligence. Will this cause the whole effort—to turn the murder of Skripal and his daughter against Russia—to backfire?

Zepp-LaRouche: This demonstrates, as never before, the role of the British, and that's a very useful thing. Those in our audience, who have been familiar with the LaRouche movement for a longer time, will

DOD/EJ Hersom

Stratcom Commander, Air Force General John E. Hyten.

remember that my husband, Lyndon LaRouche, was always attacked for having pointed to the role of the British, the British empire—which still exists, though not in its old form. The British empire now exists in the form of the leading financial institutions, and the whole system of private security firms, and the central bank/insurance company system. The trans-Atlantic financial structure **is** the present form of the British empire. My husband pointed to the fact that it is that system which is at the core of the corruption in the United States, and runs much of the dope traffic. He has been repeatedly attacked for saying that the British monarchy is behind all of this. Anyone who looks at the present manipulation of the situation, can now see, very clearly, the role of that British empire. Boris Johnson and Theresa May are acting as instruments of that imperial financial empire.

I think it is very useful that this is now all out in the open. The United States of America was created by the American Revolution, which was a War of Independence, for freedom from the British Empire. If you look at history, that same British Empire never gave up the idea of reconquering the United States. It succeeded, in a sense, in establishing the "special relationship" between the United States and Great Britain to run the world as a unipolar world. If President Trump breaks out of that,—and that has been the real reason for the attacks on him—and establishes direct communication with Russia and China, then that's the end of this kind of geopolitical manipulation, of divide and conquer, of the world. That would be very good, and I think that should happen, right now.

John Brennan
White House

back to protecting the privacy of its citizens? I think the idea that everything is transparent and everything is allowed, is the means to manipulate everyone. It's really means that you are giving up your individual freedom, and setting yourself up to be completely controlled, by being profiled, shaped, nudged,—nudged into any direction. I think people should reflect on all of this, and not be so absolutely naive.

This Cambridge Analytica story and the role of Facebook is a very useful revelation, a reminder to think about these matters in a different way.

Schlanger: When we talk about backfiring, this calls to mind something you often bring up, Schiller's idea of the "Ibykus principle." We see this happening with Russiagate, in the firing of FBI Deputy Director Andrew McCabe in the last days and the new focus on former CIA Director John Brennan. There have just been a whole series of articles attacking John Brennan, who openly said that Trump is crazy and that he has to be removed. Then, there's a whole story of the attempt to ensnare Trump in these Cambridge Analytica revelations. There's a whole different story, however, that's now coming out on this. This is the Ibykus principle, isn't it?

Zepp-LaRouche: Yes and it's very useful. We have, for a long time now, warned of the danger of young people becoming addicted to the so-called "social media," in which real life, real friendships, and real discussions are replaced by an almost autistic dependency on the so-called social media, which is a virtual reality in which so-called "friends" are not friends. It turns out that this whole thing was simply a commercial operation to collect private data and then sell it to commercial and other interests. It is very useful that this is now out in the open.

A comment by Edward Snowden, in this context, is also very interesting. He said: A firm which collects and sells private data should be rightly called a surveillance institution. Calling those firms "social media" is the most successful fraud since the story that the War Ministry is really a Defense Ministry was officially sold to the public.

This whole affair should lead people to rethink these questions. What do you do about this surveillance apparatus? How do you trust this? How do you re-establish privacy control? How do you control the use of private data, and force government and its legislators to go

Schlanger: Then you have the other irony which came to the surface in the efforts by the media to pin Press Secretary Sarah Sanders down on why Trump didn't talk about fraud in the Russian elections. She made the comment that, "We're not in the business of telling other countries how to run their elections." However, it does seem as though we completely—by "we" I mean the United States government—constantly talk about Russian government interference in the private lives of Russians, when, what Snowden showed, and Clapper unsuccessfully lied to cover up, is that the biggest violator is the U.S. National Security Agency!

Now, on the Ibykus principle, Helga, I don't know if

we have enough on this yet for you to say much, but it should be noted that former French President Nicolas Sarkozy was arrested yesterday, one day after the seventh anniversary of his role in working together with then British Prime Minister David Cameron, and also with Obama and Hillary Clinton, to destroy Libya and kill Qaddafi. Do you have anything on that story?

Zepp-LaRouche: I have to see what our French colleagues have on that. But I can tell you this much: The story is widely being discussed in Italy. Many former politicians are now commenting on it, saying that it was a big mistake for Italy to be drawn into this war—by the British and Hillary Clinton—who then convinced NATO, and then drew Italy in to join in the attack on Libya. These Italian figures are now saying that they should have instead discussed this more seriously with Germany at the time.

German Foreign Minister Guido Westerwelle had refused to go along with the NATO military intervention in Libya, in 2011.

What these Italian politicians are pointing to—if the accusations are true, which does need to be determined—is that Sarkozy received a large amount of money from Qaddafi. Qaddafi's son and a former adviser to Qaddafi have now testified that Sarkozy had demanded $50 million for his election campaign and Qaddafi did give him $20 million. Later Sarkozy—according to the Italian media and some politicians—engaged France in his personal warfare against Qaddafi, to eliminate a witness. If that is true, that is, indeed, stupendous. These Italian politicians, including a former deputy secretary of defense, are saying that this war led to a complete destruction of Libya, that terrible economic, social and humanitarian catastrophes have erupted because of that NATO intervention. The whole Libyan state is still completely torn apart. The refugee crisis, and the impact of it on Italy, in terms of the refugees, in terms of energy supplies and so forth, is also quite devastating.

But, this is just one more symptom among many. If you look at what has come out in terms of the political class, managers, and academia,—there have never been

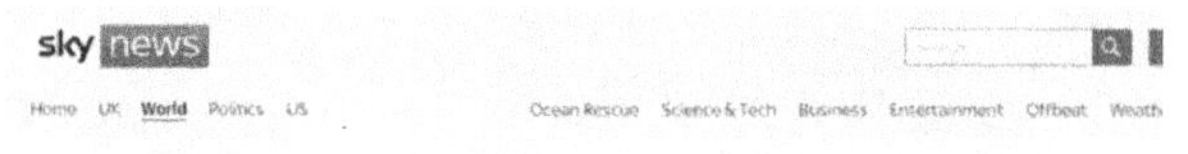

Ex-French president Nicolas Sarkozy arrested over campaign financing

The Former French president is being questioned in connection to alleged Libyan funding for his 2007 election campaign.

so many disgraceful representatives of the so-called "elite" and establishment. I think it is a very serious problem we have in the West. In Europe, it is the reason for the growth of some of these xenophobic right-wing populist parties. There is, at the same time, a complete collapse and disappearance of the so-called people's parties which are being replaced by populist movements or extreme right-wing movements. That is a serious reflection of the real moral crisis of the West.

That's why we need a change; we need a New Paradigm. We are calling on you, you our viewers, to help. Enter into discourse with us: Where should our future be? Why do we need a New Paradigm?

Schlanger: We should remind our listeners that Hillary Clinton played a big role in the Libya operation, and this was one of the points that President Trump focussed on, when he said that this administration would stop regime-change policies.

Now, let's move away from this discussion of the corruption of the establishment in the West. Let's move to something much more positive. You brought up the New Paradigm: President Xi Jinping just gave the closing speech at the "two sessions" conferences in China, in which he reiterated the long-term goals for China in his Presidency, and I'd like your thoughts on what he had to say there.

Zepp-LaRouche: Well, first of all, he emphasized both humility and pride. He said the purpose of leadership is to serve the people. He repeated that many times, and thanked the Chinese population for having the confidence to allow him to continue his leadership. The Western media is completely upset about Xi Jinping being now in a leadership position for an indefinite period into the future. From a Chinese standpoint, Xi Jinping has proven to be an exceptional leader. Xi said, this is going to be a very difficult period for China, because it takes place in a very complex world situation, and he, indeed, called for a new "Long March." This is quite an amazing historic reference to the history of China.

He is clearly somebody who is devoted to the

common good of the Chinese people. Consider what China is actually doing, and how the Chinese people are happy to have such a leader. The Russian people are similarly happy to have Putin; after all, the 76% vote for Putin is much more than the West expected. There is a very funny way to look at these events in Russia: "Oh, Putin won the election—and the Russians did it!" I find it amusing, with all of this Russia-bashing, and the claims that the Russians are behind everything.

We have a situation where Russia is clearly responding to Putin's leadership. China is clearly devoted to continuing on the course of the New Silk Road, the Belt and Road Initiative, with many more countries joining. Morgan Stanley, one of the Wall Street banks, released a report saying this is the largest infrastructure project in history and it will continue, it will make China a very strong, modern economy with wealthy inhabitants, and all the countries that join will experience the same result. The report says that the Asian Infrastructure Investment Bank has estimated that there is an infrastructure financing gap of about $21 trillion. This is an enormous task to accomplish. The previous leading financial institutions of the West, the IMF and World Bank, did not provide that kind of development financing. China is uplifting the developing countries, which is actually priceless. For the first time, these countries have a chance to truly overcome their underdevelopment and widespread poverty, which has been really terrible.

That is very good. The New Silk Road Spirit is something that people need to understand. It's based on the idea of the harmonious development of all nations, working together for the mutual benefit of all people. China is, of course, pursuing its own interests, but the other countries working with the Belt and Road Initiative are quite happy. For the first time, their interests are being seriously considered, and developed, as well.

The whole propaganda war against China is based on nothing but lies. It's naked propaganda coming from geopolitical warmongering people in the West. We should build a mass movement of people who say "no" to these lies. We should take up the offer of Xi Jinping and have win-win cooperation and join the New Silk

Xinhua/Xie Huanchi

President of China Xi Jinping, at a panel discussion with deputies from Inner Mongolia, at the 13th National People's Congress on March 5, 2018.

Road projects. There are plenty of tasks for us to join; we can participate in the common destiny of mankind. Xi Jinping, in this speech, used a very beautiful idea, "Let the Sun shine on the shared community for the one future of humanity."

Schlanger: In contrast to the positive report from Morgan Stanley on China, the chief market economist for Goldman Sachs, Charles Himmelberg, warned of the financial fragility in the West, especially if liquidity flows are cut. Yesterday the Federal Reserve Board met and said it's going to cut liquidity flows by raising interest rates another three to five times over the next twelve months! So I think we can see the contrast very clearly.

Now one of the other areas where a contrast comes in, is that in spite of the threats from the anti-China lobby in the United States about the "danger" of China becoming a hegemonic power, there are continuing, positive developments on the Korean Peninsula, which include collaboration between President Trump and Xi Jinping. There are a couple of summits that were announced. Helga, it looks as though this is going to continue to build toward the possibility of an outbreak of peace.

Zepp-LaRouche: Yes. It is now very likely that there will be a trilateral summit in May, between Trump, Kim Jong-un, and President Moon Jae-in of South Korea. There will be other meetings involving Japan and Russia. I think there is a strategic realignment going on.

The countries that are stubbornly insisting on geo-

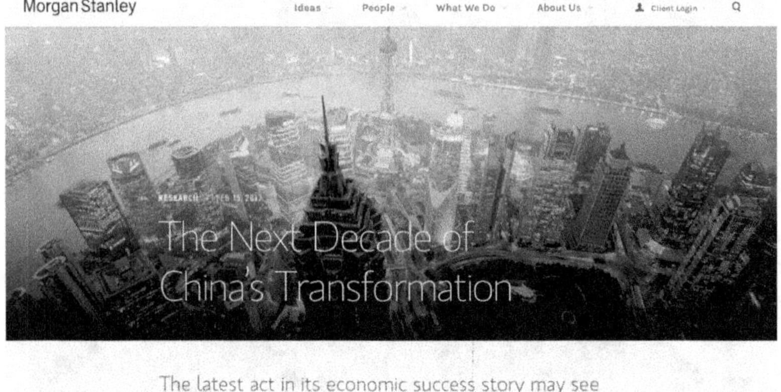

Morgan Stanley report: "The Next Decade of China's Transformation."

political confrontation will be sidelined. I'm not underestimating the danger, as we can see by the British behavior, but I think the overwhelming tendency is really development and cooperation, and this is very good.

Let me just mention one last point on this contrast. China is cooperating with many African nations, building railways and industrial projects. We have spoken in these broadcasts about the beautiful Transaqua project, which is now on the table; this is bringing the Silk Road Spirit into Africa.

The reason I am mentioning this, is that the neoliberal/neo-con geopolitical system is really not out for win-win. It exploits its own advantages. The fact that the EU is doing that is really one more reason to say that it represents a system which is not in the interest of anybody it cooperates with, nor in the interest of its own members. If you need proof, just look at the southern European countries, which have been completely smashed by the austerity policies of the Troika. I think that what we need instead is exactly what Italy is now doing—working with China and the African nations in building up real economic development like the Transaqua project.

I think we have a crystal clear picture in which you see the intentions of the two paradigms—the old paradigm of neoliberal control of the world, and the New Paradigm of harmonious development of all nations. People should join with us to help make sure that the second one becomes victorious.

Schlanger: Helga, speaking about being stuck in the old paradigm: Do you have anything to say about the new appointments to the new German government?

Zepp-LaRouche: That is a very sad story. Mrs. Merkel has had nothing better to do than act as the puppy dog of the British. This is disgraceful. It should be well noted and understood by everybody.

The SPD is also in a deep crisis. It has fallen in the preference polls to less than 15%. What did the new Finance Minister Olaf Scholz do? He appointed a banker from Goldman Sachs, Jörg Kukies, to be deputy finance minister, and that has caused a revolt in the German population. There was a poll reporting that 64.9% of the people thought this was disgusting. He also appointed Werner Gatzer, who is known to be the architect of the hated "black zero" (no deficit) policy of former Finance Minister Schäuble. Scholz then reported that he's happy that he was able to put together a good team.

That is a foreboding development for Germany. As most people know, we are on the verge of a new financial crash. Sheila Bair, the former head of the FDIC in the United States, warned of the consequences of the continuation of the derivatives trade and speculative excesses. This non-correction of the causes of the 2008 crisis means we face the danger of a new, even bigger crash. She contrasted those dangerous policies with what China has been doing, in its efforts to completely forbid speculative investments, and stabilize the banking sector by increasing required bank reserves to 15%.

Having a pro-bubble government in Germany is not good. There are many Italian politicians from the Lega and the Five Star Party who are calling for Glass-Steagall. The EU is trying, in stark contrast, to promote a Five Star-Democratic Party coalition government, which would be, from their standpoint, the best option to preserve this speculative system.

I'm emphasizing this because the Damocles Sword of a new financial crash is still hanging over the world. Given the fact that China has tried to move its financial system into safe waters, it is probably better protected against the effects of such a crisis than anybody else.

Join us, work with the Schiller Institute to mobilize for the Four Laws proposed by my husband, Lyndon LaRouche: Glass-Steagall, a return to Hamiltonian banking; a credit system and National Bank; a science-driver program for thermonuclear fusion research and power, cooperation in space exploration. Let us all join the New

Silk Road countries so that we can, very rapidly, have a New Paradigm in the world. But it requires you. And it requires people to become active and not leave mankind in the hands of a corrupt establishment.

Schlanger: Helga, I think we can conclude by coming to the commemoration of an event which proved that cynics—people who say you can't change the world with big ideas—are not right. Thirty-five years ago, on March 23, 1983, there was a shock effect around the world, when Ronald Reagan gave a prime-time speech, at the end of which he endorsed the policy, which your husband, Lyndon LaRouche, first introduced with his pamphlet "Sputnik of the '70s."—that is, the Strategic Defense Initiative. And it's especially relevant today, given what we're seeing from Russia and President Putin. So I'd like your reflections on the importance of the anniversary of this event from 35 years ago.

Zepp-LaRouche: The SDI proposal was grossly mischaracterized by the media, by calling it "Star Wars," and things like that. My husband's SDI proposal was a farsighted, clear vision of a New Paradigm. I strongly suggest you read more about it, especially the proposed draft for a dialogue among the superpowers, which was published one year later. You can find his memorandum in the *Executive Intelligence Review*, "The LaRouche Doctrine: A Draft Memorandum for an Agreement between the United States of America and the U.S.S.R.," which was published on April 17, 1984. This is a proposal for both superpowers to develop together, new physical principles that would make nuclear weapons obsolete. Putin's March 1 speech, which presented new weapons systems based on new physical principles, is absolutely in this tradition. Putin also asked for new discussions to negotiate and put together a new security architecture, including Russia, the United States, China, and the Europeans.

This was all envisioned by my husband in this famous SDI proposal. It was a very far-reaching proposal to dissolve the blocs—NATO and the Warsaw Pact—to have instead cooperation among sovereign re-

1977 LaRouche movement pamphlet.

publics, which is exactly what the New Silk Road dynamic today represents. And it was also the idea to use a science-driver in the economy to use the increased productivity of the real economy for extensive technology transfers to the developing sector, in order to overcome their underdevelopment and poverty.

This is what we're seeing today, also, in the collaboration between China, Russia and the countries that are participating in the Belt and Road Initiative.

In a certain sense, part of this potential of peace breaking out, so feared by the British empire, is that there is right now the very vivid tradition—and actualization of that tradition—of the SDI. I think we should circulate this proposal by my husband again. I think we should enlarge it to become the SDE, the Strategic Defense of the Earth. It was just discovered that very soon, another big asteroid will be on course taking it very close to Earth. So we need to move quickly to the common aims of mankind. All countries should cooperate and become a shared community for the one future of humanity.

This is the New Paradigm which I think should be obvious. If you look at the long arc of history, we *have* to overcome geopolitics and we have to move to a kind of cooperation where we put all our forces together to solve those questions which are a challenge to all of humanity—nuclear weapons, poverty, asteroids—there are so many areas where we could fruitfully cooperate—space exploration is one of them. And I think we are in a very fascinating moment in history, but we need more active citizens: So please contact us, work with us, and let's together make a better world.

Schlanger: I think that's a very good place to end. People should now realize that giving up your pessimism is one of the keys to bringing online this new paradigm.

So, Helga, thank you very much for joining us today, and we'll see you next week.

Zepp-LaRouche: Yes, see you next week.

hz.zepp@schiller-institut.de

What is the SDE, and Why Do We Need it Now?

by Stephanie Ezrol

March 25—In 1957, mankind launched the first artificial satellite in orbit around the Earth. We quickly confirmed with the next 60 years of space exploration that there is no empty space out there, but instead there are belts of radiation, solar winds, and varied fields of radiation as well as a constant flow of asteroids, comets and assorted space debris sharing the 239,000 miles of territory between us on Earth, and the Moon.

In the sixty years since 1957, we have vastly expanded our understanding of our surroundings, including threats to the well-being and even the continuing existence of life on Earth. We also now know that our sun's domain extends far beyond the 7.4 billion km furthest distance of Pluto and to the possibly 30 trillion km distant Oort cloud, believed to be the source of potentially planet-threatening comets.

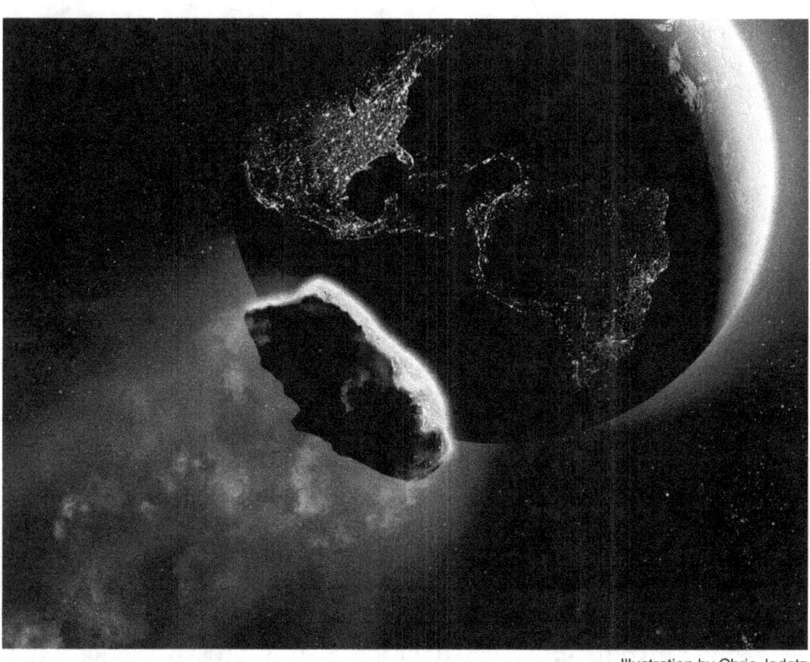

Illustration by Chris Jadatz

Artist's rendition of a threat to Earth from space.

R. Mewaldt & P. Liewer, JPL, NASA

Artist's depiction of the hypothesized Oort cloud distribution of cometary bodies populating the farthest reaches of the Solar System.

The Strategic Defense of Earth (SDE) is an extension and expansion of Lyndon LaRouche's project to replace the insane military doctrine of Mutually Assured Destruction, aptly named MAD, with Mutually Assured Survival, based on the development of space-based beam and laser devices using new physical principles which would render nuclear weapons impotent and obsolete. That was President Reagan's Strategic Defense Initiative (SDI).

The SDE emerged, in post-communist Russia, as a proposal for joint Russian and NATO development of a global system of defense against missiles, asteroids, comets and other space-based threats to the Earth. Dmitri Rogozin, then the Russian ambassador to NATO and now the Deputy Prime Minister in charge of the defense and space industries, proposed the SDE in 2011 "to overcome the Russia-U.S. deadlock over the missile defense," according to a contemporaneous report in Russia Today. It described the SDE as "a new initiative: a global system to guard against missiles—as well as asteroids and other threats from space."

Helga Zepp-LaRouche, in her March 22 Schiller Institute weekly webcast (this issue, page 26), called for enlarging Lyndon LaRouche's 1984 "Draft Memorandum for an Agreement between the United States of America and the U.S.S.R." to "become the SDE." The Schiller Institute sponsored a conference on March 23, 2013 on this very subject. Benjamin Deniston, in a 30 minute multi-media presentation, presented the stark picture of the threat to Earth from "near-earth objects" (NEOs) the vast majority of which are too small for us to see but large enough to create widespread damage.

Explosion of the asteroid over Chelyabinsk, Russia, February 15, 2013.

The urgency of the SDE is underscored by recent events. In the last 110 years, we have experienced the incredible damage of the impact of such un-seeable small space rocks. The 1908 Tunguska Event, is the most modern destructive evidence of such impact. What was most probably an asteroid traveling at about 15 km per second exploded over Siberia with a power estimated to be hundreds of times that of the bomb dropped on Hiroshima. That blast destroyed about 800 square miles of forest, flattened about 80 million trees, and left hundreds of burnt reindeer carcasses. On Feb. 15, 2013 a relatively small asteroid exploded over Chelyabinsk, Russia with a blast equivalent to more than 300,000 tons of TNT, shattering windows for miles, injuring more than 1,000 people, and damaging 3,000 buildings. This was the "most energetic impact event recognized since the 1908 Tunguska blast," according the Jet Propulsion Laboratory's Center for Near Earth Object Studies.

To truly face and defeat such dangers, and the threat to civilization of hits from comets or asteroids in the kilometer-sized range, we must now become a space-faring people. To see what we can't see, we will need to be on the Moon, and on planets beyond the Moon. To control and develop our 239,000-mile neighborhood between the Earth and the Moon, we will need to be able to build and launch ships from the Moon. As General Douglas MacArthur so clearly presented the need for a New Paradigm of human relations on Sept. 2, 1945 aboard the Battleship Missouri, in the age of nuclear weapons, war is no longer an option. MacArthur said then, "If we will not devise some greater and more equitable system, Armageddon will be at our door. The problem basically is theological and involves a spiritual recrudescence and improvement of human character that will synchronize with our almost matchless advances in science, art, literature, and all material and cultural developments of the past 2,000 years. It must be of the spirit if we are to save the flesh."

The LaRouche Political Action Committee and the Schiller Institute both have in-depth multi-media material available for studying and teaching this most urgent subject. Human beings were built with the capacity to constantly transcend limits. We don't need to kill each other, we need to take on the real challenges with the intellectual and spiritual strength inherent in our very being.

Known Near-Earth Asteroids

January 1980-June 2012

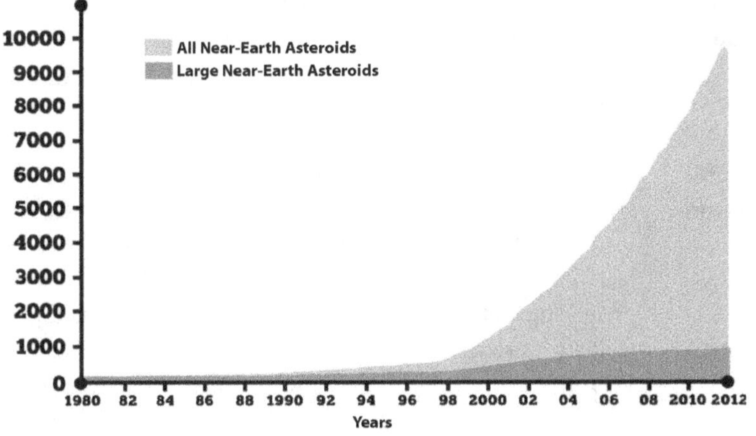

China's People's Congress Moves To Implement New Era Policies

by William Jones

March 25—The annual meeting of China's two law-making bodies, the National People's Congress (NPC) and the Chinese People's Political Consultative Conference (CPPCC), garnered more international attention than usual this year. What grabbed the most media notice was the decision by the NPC, China's legislature, to eliminate the two-term limits for the country's President and Vice President. This means effectively that China's President Xi Jinping can again serve as president after the end of his present term in 2022. There was a good deal of speculation as to why this was done; most of the Western media characteristically attributed it to sinister motives.

Xinhua/Li Xin

A press conference on poverty alleviation at the 13th National People's Congress on March 7, 2018.

But what was more significant about the "Two Sessions," as these two annual meetings are called, was the consolidation of the new policy that had been clearly formulated at last year's 19th Communist Party Congress, which called for a new direction in China's development policy and a new and formative role for China in the international arena, policies which have been developed under the aegis of Xi Jinping.

China's Reform and Deng's Caveat

The world has been amazed at the rapidity with which China has developed during the last 40 years since Deng Xiaoping launched his "reform and opening up" in 1978, which helped pull China out of the catastrophe of the Cultural Revolution, in which the intellectual and professional elite of China had been decimated.

Deng's leadership helped restore sanity to Chinese policy, and began an era of opening up to the outside world which provided the momentum for rebuilding Chinese society. But a subsidiary aspect of Deng's policy was a caveat not to "make waves" internationally. "Hide your strength and bide your time" was how he put it. China, Deng said, should proceed to quietly build up the scientific and intellectual capabilities which would allow it to eventually emerge from its "entry level" into the world economy as a low-wage producer for the Western economies, and to go on to transform itself into a modern and "moderately prosperous society."

Some among the Chinese elites, fueled by the exaggerated wishes of some Western political circles, believed that China would "morph" into a placid, and totally subordinate, member of the Western "international order" In fact, during the 1980s, when China was trying to acclimatize itself to the Western system, they would invite leading intellectuals from the West and from Eastern Europe (which had developed its own form of

Deputy Premier of China Deng Xiaoping, being briefed by Christopher Kraft, the director of the Johnson Space Center.

Charting a New Path for China

By 2013, it was becoming clear which road China had to take. The announcement of the Silk Road Economic Belt by President Xi Jinping in September 2013 in Astana, Kazakhstan, was the launching of a new economic policy, based on the willingness of China to make major infrastructure investments abroad intended to foster growth and development. The investments initially focused on China's immediate neighbors in Central Asia and Southeast Asia, but quickly spread beyond the immediate neighborhood to a large part of the developing world. And China's continued identification with, and sympathy for the other developing countries, created a keen sense of solidarity with the plight of these nations.

With its Belt and Road Initiative, China stepped out onto the world stage in a big way. On the one hand, it raised the profile of China as a major power pursuing an independent policy. The policy was greeted enthusiastically by most developing countries, who now saw a possible way out of the continual cycle of poverty and crisis, and even by many of the developed countries, which saw in it a means of reviving their own faltering economies. Many among the Western elites, however, viewed the Belt and Road as a threat to a system in which *they* set the rules.

And while China was prepared to take its place as a responsible party in the post-World War II international institutions, upholding the rules of the UN, the WTO, and other international organizations, it nevertheless felt that its ideas about development through increased participation with Western institutions, and infrastructural development, were far superior to the way the world had been operating over the previous two decades. And its clear recognition of the ever-present danger of a blow-out of the bloated international debt system, led it to call for major economic reforms at the international level.

While Xi Jinping's new orientation no doubt met with some internal opposition from those in China who still felt that China should maintain a low profile, during the course of the last five years President Xi has largely succeeded in overcoming that opposition, and has, in fact, imbued the nation with a new sense of patriotism in support of this new policy. And the new policy also entails, as President Xi has continually pointed out, a

"goulash Communism"), to advise them on how to reform the Chinese system in order to better comply with the rules of Western-style "capitalism."

Needless to say, not all Chinese leaders were happy with such a direction. After all, the Communist Party was supposed to be devoted to the interests of the workers and peasants, not to the wishes of a growing middle class which had succeeded in working its way out of poverty. But the extraordinary economic successes resulting from the policy of adaptation served to quiet any dissent along these lines.

The first shock to this outlook came with the demise of the Soviet Union. The Soviets had also "opened up" their economies to Western capitalism. They had privatized their industries and allowed the untrammeled entry of Western capitalists into their midst. But it had brought down the entire structure and crushed Russia. But even more, it was the major global financial crisis of 2008 which really made it clear to Chinese leaders that this system was seriously flawed, and would not lead to a successful outcome for China as it became more and more integrated into that system. There had to be a new direction and China had to find out what it was.

transition from geopolitics, with its cut-throat competition and its zero-sum solutions, to a policy of mutual benefit and the creation of a "community of shared interest for humanity." He has also been insistent that the developing countries must have a greater say in the shaping of the future of this new community.

At the recent Two Sessions, Xi's basic concept, under the rubric of "Socialism with Chinese Characteristics for a New Era," was overwhelmingly accepted and written into the country's constitution. It had similarly been written into the Communist Party constitution at the end of last year.

At the same time, there was a clear emphasis at the Two Sessions on the crucial, leading role of the Communist Party of China (PRC). The party has ruled China for almost 70 years (next year will be the 70th anniversary of the founding of the People's Republic of China). Most of what has been accomplished in China since that time has been the result of the work of the ruling party. But readers should be aware that there are other parties in China, as there have been since the founding of the PRC, and many of their members participated in the Two Sessions. President Xi met with their leaders a number of times at the conference to explain the new direction the country was taking, and he urged them to give their full support to the CPC in that effort.

The meeting of the Congress also provided the opportunity to put into leading positions people whom President Xi knew were totally in agreement with this new "going out" perspective. Yet there were still those who feared that China's heightened international profile might become a target for criticism from the Western countries, particularly from the British and the Americans, but not only them.

There were also elements within the Communist Party that were not entirely favorable to Xi's leadership. This was particularly the case when he started to move against corruption. When the Chinese economy had begun to grow during the "reform and opening up" period, this growth also provided many people with excellent opportunities to strike it rich—as Deng had somewhat laconically advised them to do—and many

Xinhua/Li Xueren

Opening meeting of the 13th National Committee of the Chinese People's Political Consultative Conference, on March 3, 2018.

did. This bred a good deal of corruption. The campaign Xi launched several years ago against corruption in the government and in the party, targeting both the high and low, both "tigers" and "flies," was aimed at bringing the party back to its commitment to Sun Yat-Sen's principle of "the People's Livelihood." The anti-corruption campaign had led to imprisonment for many leading officials, no doubt ruffling the feathers of their friends as well.

With a view to preventing further corruption from tarnishing the government and the party, the Congress agreed to set up a Supervisory Commission, which will operate at all government levels: central, provincial, and district, in order to monitor any deviation towards corruption by party or government officials. While much of the corruption has already been eliminated, President Xi is determined that it not again become a problem.

Backed by the new leadership coming out of the recent National People's Congress, President Xi can be assured that he has the support of the party for moving further in the direction outlined by him in this new era.

Chinese Socialism in the New Era

The ultimate goal, as now outlined in the Constitution by one of the amendments passed by the NPC, is to achieve by 2050 a "great modern socialist country that is prosperous, strong, democratic, culturally advanced, harmonious, and beautiful." This phrase was also added to the new oath of office, introduced by Xi and established by the NPC, which every government official must now take. At his re-election as president, President Xi himself became the first person to take that oath.

And in his final speech to the National People's Congress, President Xi was quite explicit about the orientation required of government and party officials in this People's Republic. "China is a socialist country of people's democratic dictatorship under the leadership of the working class based on an alliance of workers and farmers," Xi told the delegates. "It is a country where all power of the state belongs to the people. We must base our efforts on the interests of the people, ensure the principal status of the people, humbly learn from the people, and heed their needs and draw on their wisdom.... We must also ensure that all Chinese people can share the happiness and pride in the historic course of national rejuvenation." The poverty reduction program set into motion by President Xi is a clear example of the direction he intends to move, in orienting government policy toward advancing the welfare of the people.

President Barack Obama at the East Asia Summit in Cambodia, Nov. 20, 2012.

But, despite China's success in lifting between 700 and 800 million people out of poverty over the last two decades, and launching the most ambitious infrastructure program in the world for dozens of neighboring and distant nations, there is still growing animosity from the British financial "lords of London"—and their faction among their American junior partners—who fear that the growth of China will radically change the world that they have for so long controlled. And they are no doubt correct. Eliminating poverty and centering development on infrastructural investment, have never been strong points of the banking elites, who preferred to clip their coupons of profits squeezed out of the labor of underpaid workers in some of the poorest countries of the world.

The Chinese leadership is fully aware of the threat posed by this international opposition. The "pivot to Asia" of Barack Obama, and the continued efforts by the U.S. Pacific Command to keep the South China Sea from any peaceful resolution of the various existing territorial claims, have clearly reflected the views of the financial elites. And while the election of Donald Trump was generally seen in China as a sign that the United States might be amenable to integrating China's program into a broader global world, a "community of shared interests," they are also aware that there are forces at work in Washington aiming at sabotaging any such development.

Countering Possible Threats

The measures taken at the People's Congress, including eliminating term limits for the president and vice president, and the strengthening of the role of the Chinese Communist Party, were undertaken to facilitate the achievement of the Two Centenary Goals (poverty elimination by 2020 and a fully developed socialist society by 2050). They are also aimed at strengthening the political structure against any possible attempts at destabilization by hostile Western interests, as was done in Ukraine earlier, which they now see unfolding against Russia, their most important partner in the Belt and Road, and a major country with whom they are in agreement on most overriding international issues.

While President Xi has clearly indicated that the "reform and opening up" will not only continue, but also expand, with more foreign industries being allowed to establish operations in China, with the help of its government—still, necessary precautions will be taken to prevent that "openness" from becoming an entry point for hostile operations.

China is rightly proud of the system that has brought the country to this point. While President Xi has indicated in his comments at the People's Con-

Xinhua

China President Xi Jinping swearing the new oath to the Constitution, March 2018.

into focus for the general public and the intelligentsia, in order to deepen and enhance the traditional thinking within party and government circles. This was also underlined in Xi's concluding remarks to the People's Congress, in which he outlined a broad sweep of the achievements of Chinese culture over the last 5,000 years. "The Chinese people are people with great creativity," Xi told the delegates. "During the thousands of years of history, the Chinese people have always been laboring, innovating, and creating with diligence. Our country has been the birthplace of world-renowned great thinkers.... The Chinese people's magnificent scientific achievements, such as paper-making, gunpowder, printing, and the compass, have profoundly influenced the progress of human civilization," Xi said.

As China transforms itself into an innovation-based economy—"innovation" and "creativity" being major themes at the Congress—the opening to the outside world is even more important to its own development today. At the same time, conscious of the growing instability in the Western financial markets, the Congress has also taken decisive measures to place oversight of insurance operations and financial operations into a single regulatory body, in order to monitor and control possible "hot money" flows into the country or other financial "machinations" that may threaten the Chinese financial system.

People in the West have got to understand that China will change and develop economically and socially in accordance with the changing needs and desires of the Chinese people, not in accordance with some outside dictate by those who wish to impose any alien template on them. And while other countries will probably not adopt the particular "Chinese model" of governance, (which China has clearly said they are not interested in exporting), there are no doubt lessons to be learned, by developed as well as developing countries, from the success that China has achieved. Perhaps if the Western countries were prepared to accept President Xi's proposal of building "a community of shared interest," they would find important elements in Chinese policies which would be beneficial for their own nations. Perhaps we might even hark back to that period in the 17th century which saw the first "opening up" of China to the arriving Jesuit astronomers and philosophers, where the beginnings of a similar, mutually beneficial "dialogue of cultures," as now lies within our grasp, began to bear fruit, and benefitted, at least for a century or so, both East and West.

gress that China would create "a socialist democracy" as it moves toward its Two Centenary Goals, it will certainly not be some mirror-image of the democratic systems as practiced in the West, systems which have revealed so many serious flaws in the last two decades. The commitment of the Chinese Government and the Chinese Communist Party to the people's livelihood is more determined than ever under the new leadership. And the fact that President Xi will no doubt be at the rudder of the ship of state even after his present term ends, gives an added degree of stability to that commitment.

President Xi has also broadened the intellectual basis for the development of "socialism with Chinese characteristics" by reviving, as a living tradition, the great thinkers throughout Chinese history, from Confucius and Mencius to the great poets of the Song and Ming dynasties. While this tradition was labeled as "rightist" and suppressed during the disastrous Cultural Revolution, it has always remained a critical element of Chinese thought and practice. And President Xi has, in his own speeches and writings, served to bring these ideas back

III. The Common Aims of Mankind

Thursday, August 16, 2012

EDWARD TELLER WAS RIGHT AT ERICE

The Threat Against Mankind

by Lyndon H. LaRouche, Jr.

The following article was authored by Lyndon LaRouche in August 2012, nearly twelve years into the Presidencies of George W. Bush and Barack Obama and during the midst of Obama's campaign for a second term. The murderous intent of the Obama Presidency had already been demonstrated with the murder of Muammar Gaddafi in 2011, and the strategic war escalation against Russia would soon take a major leap forward with the UK/U.S.-sponsored coup in the Ukraine in 2014. Since that time, however, a major strategic shift has occurred in the world, beginning with the October 2013 launching of the China-sponsored Belt and Road Initiative, a project which brings to the forefront of global policy precisely the scientific and economic perspective for which Lyndon LaRouche has been the leading spokesman for more than forty years. The strategic situation has changed since 2012. Yet, the economic, cultural, and scientific issues which LaRouche addresses, particularly in the second half of this report, beginning with the section "The LaRouche Factor," remain as critical challenges to be addressed.

The following is a report bearing upon the current prospects for the survival of mankind. I include within it, not only the consideration of presently crucial trends and developments, but add, and will conclude with some necessary, deeper references to the roots of these matters of forecasting, with emphasis on roots dating from the late 1950s through the 1970s and 1980s.

The first issue of principle to be kept in mind, in reading the report as a whole, is the pathological implications of reliance on the intrinsically incompetent, but still popular, statistical-mathematical modes of economic forecasting. However, let us come to that point in the history of this process in due course. First, let us consider the immediate crisis-situation itself.

At this present moment, there are two mutually contradictory options respecting the continued survival of the human species. One, is typified by the present lurch toward virtually global thermonuclear war, an option which is presently centered in the strategic policies of either U.S. President Barack Obama himself, or someone using Obama as if he were a mere puppet. The only realistic choice of alternative to that at the present point of the trans-Atlantic economic-breakdown crisis, would be the triple-point package which I have presented as what would be the only presently available alternative to a currently onrushing economic breakdown crisis:

1. *Immediate re-enactment of President Franklin Roosevelt's 1933 Glass-Steagall Act.*
2. *Replacing the presently hopelessly bankrupt, present U.S. monetarist system, by a banking system based on the principle of national credit.*
3. *The immediate launching of a modern replication (NAWAPA XXI) of the original NAWAPA program of management of North American water-resources, estimated to provide 4 million skilled places of employment, as supplemented by an additional 2 million other high-quality machine-tool-grade and closely related places of employment, including the re-establishment of a "full throttle" NASA program for defense of Earth in the range of Mars-orbit and beyond.*

The Following Policies Must Be Established:

Were Obama to succeed in his prospective candidacy for a second term in office, two consequences were the likely ones: (a) thermonuclear warfare is more or less an immediate likelihood, and, (b) a near-extinction of the human species might be reasonably expected to occur either soon after President Obama's renomination, or not distant from the time of his actual re-election. Under those two conditions, human life on this planet could not be reasonably expected to escape the actual, or virtual near-doom of mankind which an actually needless thermonuclear war between the U.S.A. and Obama's presently continuing list of designated targets implies. That list has included: nations such as Libya (already done by lawbreaker Obama), Syria, and Iran (actively targeted now), and includes the thermonuclear powers Russia and China as intended targets for a thermonuclear war launched as the nominal intention of a President Obama.

I must add to that list of threats, the cowardice which I have recently witnessed from so many U.S. citizens on that account. That still surprises me, but only with its enormity, once all were considered in the light of all those relevant factors which I have seen since the assassinations of President John F. Kennedy and his brother Robert. "How were it possible, that thinking adult citizens of the United States would even imagine that Obama's intention is not the inception of thermonuclear warfare against a group of targeted nations including Russia, China and others?" It would be a war launched with full-blast qualities of thermonuclear blows, on both sides. It would be a war, which would represent a commitment to virtual extinction of the present world population, either by the attacks themselves, or as the aftermath expressed as the fruit of the consequences facing every part of this planet after an opening of full-scale exchange of fire, by and against both Obama and his selected targets. How dumb (or, simply cowardly) could so many among our nation's putative leaders have become!?

Such a war as that which Barack Obama has implicitly demanded of the U.S.A., as since his unlawful

Thermonuclear war would mean the near-extension of the human species. These photos from Nagasaki (a rare ground-level photo during the bombing) and Hiroshima (afterwards) give a sense of the power of the fission bomb; the fusion bomb is many orders of magnitude more devastating.

U.S. National Archives

Libya atrocity, would mean, in its effects, the virtually inevitable extinction of the human species on Earth. Who, then, could be so dumb or silly, then, as to wish his re-election? Above all else, Obama must go into a forced retirement tantamount to what should have been his impeachment long since, while there were still a living human species in our republic to defend. Admittedly, we of the United States have fallen a long way down on the scale of moral values since heroes of the likeness of our President Franklin D. Roosevelt, or Roosevelt's martyred follower, John F. Kennedy; but, despite our self-inflicted disgrace on that account, we still have an honorable right, as human beings, to continue to exist, an existence which the continued incumbency of President Barack Obama would, according to him, deny us.

Happily, this will not be the end of the crucial mat-

ters at hand. There are at least a few good reasons for hope, as follows.

On 'Curiosity...'

With the successful arrival of "Curiosity" at its intended destination, an entirely new, hopeful state of strategic affairs has been delivered: the safe arrival of "Curiosity" at its intended destination. "Curiosity's" successful landing, now brings mankind, as a whole, to the feasibility of proceeding to organize the defense of Earth against presently existing, deadly threats to Earth from the region of space including Earth, such as Mars, and the vicinity of Venus. It gives us, among other benefits, the justified hope to believe, that the human species might find succor, whenever, and wherever it is within the reach that is needed, for the continuation of that great mission which we have yet to come to know fully.

On the other hand, one "rather awesome rock," for example, unless prevented, could mean a more or less vast destruction of some region on the surface of Earth, or even, in the extreme case, the extinction of the human species. This would include those silly victims who had insisted: "I didn't read what you are saying in any newspaper which I read." Wars fought "on the table," should not be aimed to annihilate the table itself.

Ban Oligarchism

However, "motives for peace" aside, it should have been evident, long since, that the human species was not created with the intention of gratifying those homicidal impulses which have been exhibited by a Barack Obama, as those impulses have been shown toward a Libya, and now to Syria, Iran, and others, of anyone with a temperament like Obama's own. To understand this situation, we must bring the nation's overview of its obligations in decision-making in such matters, beyond the domain of even what has been long known as that of "the oligarchical principle," and outside what have been the underlying phenomena of that specifically "oligarchical" type, already long-since typified by the case of the temperament of the original Roman Empire of creatures such as that Emperor Nero whom Obama has tended to mimic in his Hitler-like health-care policies thus far, and his habits of outright homicide thus far. The oligarchical principle must be efficiently excluded from the permitted strategic practice of nations.

As the greatest of our known poets and dramatists already knew, and historians and statesmen should have known, the oligarchical prototype is one which serves a chosen sort of a wicked master all its own. The institution of humanity which sane human beings must recognize as their proper constituency, is typified by those who are prepared to discover evidence supporting the possible past residence of the human species, or its likeness, on Mars, or beyond, a species on whose behalf we must be determined to build whatever defense might be needed on behalf of any species with the characteristics of our own.

When we will have taken adequately into account what we have come to recognize now as if our own mission, we must then recognize an implicit mission assigned to the future development of our human species, or its future likeness. It is a development arising from our devoted search for a fuller understanding of what a distant destiny would have us become. That is key to the proper morality which must guide us henceforth.

That much said by, perhaps, some ancient poet within us, turn now to the science of what is to be fairly recognized as the more awesome among the presently immediate implications of certain developments of recent decades of history, up to the present date. The present threat to the continued existance of the human species should now be clear to those thinking clearly respecting the facts of the matter: the question is, how did this present horror come about, and how might we be rid of it?

I. The Recent History of Warfare

Let us now proceed accordingly, clear-headed and at a reasonable pace. Begin with a convenient definition of the need for an unbroken link of the wishful close of what was called "World War II," other than that to be recognized as the presently organized beginning of what was to begin the long march into a presently, immediately threatened thermonuclear World War III. The attempt to launch such a war, as by U.S. President Barack Obama, is to be recognized and banned, on the premises of its nature, as the gravest of all possible crimes against humanity, as to be judged as under natural law.

We must, therefore, now consider relevant precedents and related examples.

The presently continuing threat, as by President Barack Obama presently, of mutual, threatened war of implicit self-extinction of the human species, was first set into apparently actual motion, as a proposal for nuclear war which had been proposed publicly by British Prime Minister Winston Churchill and Bertrand Russell, during the close of the Summer of 1946.

At that time, the British threat of such pre-emptive actions by those primary sources, was presumed, from and by London, to occur under the influence of the British empire's Winston Churchill and Churchill's puppet of that moment, U.S. President Harry S Truman. This was the case, when they had unleashed a far worse than merely useless, nuclear bombardment of an already hopelessly defeated Japan. General Douglas MacArthur's forces had won President Franklin Roosevelt's war in the Pacific; Churchill and Truman concluded it as a wicked farce—and new wars to come.

Then, behind this turn at that time, there was not only Churchill, but that cowardly and eternally insolent terrorist, the Bertrand Russell who declared, in September 1946, his personal commitment to the launching of a "preventive" nuclear warfare against what had been until about that time, a U.S. war-time ally, the Soviet Union.[1] At that time, Bertrand Russell et al. had proceeded under the misguided presumption that the Soviet Union did not have the ability to create and deploy even nuclear-fission weapons systems. The real targets of Churchill and of his lackey, Wall Street "maven" Harry S Truman, had implicitly presumed, that their immediate threat of nuclear warfare was to be continued for as long as Russell and others had remained confident that Russia lacked the capability to have produced a deployable nuclear arsenal.

The discovery that the Soviet Union was already in possession of nuclear combat capabilities, induced Russell et al. to postpone nuclear-fission warfare until such time that actually thermonuclear warfare would be recognized as a serious intention, on both sides of the so-called "Cold War." Then came the time a Soviet Union's adventurous Nikita Khrushchov had launched a giant nuclear package (if of questionable merit as an actual weapons system) as a threat of nuclear war: for all of which Bertrand Russell was much pleased with himself.

The real military targets of Wall Street's "trained monkey" Truman, and of Winston Churchill and Churchill's followers throughout the remaining years of Bertrand Russell's life-time, were the post-war Soviet Union, and ultimately also China. The included purpose of that hoax backed by both Wall Street "maven" President Truman and Winston Churchill, was to preserve the British empire as an off-again, on-again, world empire, in effect—with hope for sufficient backing from the U.S.A.[2] That had been the monarchy's practiced intention up through the recent days of inherently wicked creatures such as Tony Blair.

However, those intentions for nuclear warfare were only a preliminary. The death of the Soviet Union's Josef Stalin and accession of the adventurous, but also confused and desperate Nikita Khrushchov as Soviet head of state, had overlapped the London/Wall Street intention to supersede nuclear warfare with an emerging mid- 1950s intent toward *thermo*nuclear "extermination warfare."[3] Implicitly, thus, thermonuclear warfare was "on the table" as a feasible general military policy of practice during the latter half of the 1950s.

With the fall of Khrushchov, and the assassination of the President of the U.S.A., President John F. Kennedy, there had still been a hope, among many American citizens, for the continuation of the creative nature of the economic and strategic intentions of President Kennedy. The assassinations of President Kennedy, and, later, of his brother, Robert Kennedy, had actually unleashed what has been, since that time, a persisting change for the worse, even now the worst, in U.S. policy, a policy which has been since continued, in various expressions, all to a common effect, up to the present time. This decades-long decline of the U.S. economy, has been continued as an accelerating trend through the terms of the Presidencies of George H.W.

---

1. See Bertrand Russell, *The Bulletin of the Atomic Scientists*, Nos. 5-6, Sept. 1, 1946.

2. The chief effect of the role of Harry S Truman, first, as Vice-President, and then President, was to wreck what had been the potency of a United States operating under the leadership of President Franklin Roosevelt. The final, post-Franklin Roosevelt interval of World War II, and the manner in which the post-Roosevelt take-down was conducted under President Truman, up to the moment of Dwight Eisenhower's election as President, was qualitative in its effects. Later, with the convenient assassination of President John F. Kennedy, the effects soon became virtually permanent. This becomes clear, once the understanding of the meaning of the physical principle of economy, "energy-flux density" in the rate of increase of per-capita productive powers of labor, is taken into account.

3. Khrushchov rose to power through a channel which the British intelligence services created and managed under the supervision of "the most evil man of his time," Bertrand Russell. Khrushchov was neither the first, nor the last Soviet leader to serve the British imperialist interest and direction on this account. Worshipful Soviet dupes of London were often left to weep at the feet of London: "How could you in London have betrayed us in this way?" That pattern continues today in certain quarters. It were, admittedly, difficult to see the future clearly, while peering between the cheeks of a London backside; I recall, very clearly, and accurately a number of cases of this *virtù*.

Bush and Bill Clinton, and has been accelerated precipitously under the Presidencies of whining George H.W. Bush's, son, "Goof-Ball" George W., Jr., and worst of them of all so far, the murderously accelerating economic-breakdown-process instituted under President Barack Obama.[4]

The Actual War-Threat

In approaching the subject of the nuclear and related sorts of strategic threat-potentials of the late 1950s and 1960s, we must take into account the fact that the increase of intensity of weaponry of the qualities of nuclear, thermonuclear and more advanced qualities of weapons systems, converges on a point at which the means of warfare mean virtually assured human extermination. This crucial point in calculations must not be limited to the direct delivery of destructive effects of the bombardment or related means, but must consider the overriding by-product-effects of having deployed such destructive force.

For example, the present level of indicated thermonuclear exchanges among indicated forces has been al-

____

4. I have never accepted the notion that the then-recently installed Soviet dictator Yuri Andropov was "honestly duped" in the matter of his radically irrational rejection of President Ronald Reagan's intentions respecting the SDI. The evidence is to be recognized in the economic implications of Andropov's trend of policies in the direction which had been set into position by Andropov's ties to Bertrand Russell, et al. In effect, Andropov was acting as a British agent since somewhere along his peregrinations around the Hungarian crisis. The history of Andropov's political evolution since the Hungarian Revolt, tilts the pointer of history toward factors pertaining to the radical shift in Andropov's career since that time. At the time he had entered the highest office, he was documented as deeply engaged in British matters. However, Khrushchov had risen to power in the Soviet Union under similar direction and sponsorship of Bertrand Russell's arrangements. On that account, we must look deep into London's imperial reaction to the defeat of London's own puppet, the Confederacy created by the British circles which had put U.S. President Jackson into place as their chronically enraged puppet. President Abraham Lincoln's defeat of London's Confederacy puppet-system, had cleared the way for the rise of the new, Bismarck-orchestrated alliance of Russia and Germany. It was the London-orchestrated ouster of Bismarck which had set into motion several strategically crucial steps into "The First World War." It was the consequent assassination of the President of France Sadi Carnot, and, especially, the British Prince of Wales' orchestration of the Japan-Britain alliance against China and eventually Russia in the Far East, which brought matters around to the launching the Balkan War. Any competent strategist today should have realized that, first, "World War I" had actually begun with the British royal family's ouster of Bismarck in 1890, and that "World War II" was a reflex of "World War I." The state of threatened "global thermonuclear warfare" now, is to be recognized accordingly. The true science of war thus far, has been the science of the shaping of history.

ready well-understood by relevant authorities, as meaning human extinction. There are only two general classes of conditions under which we would consider the presently asserted, threat-intent against Russia and China, in particular, as having crossed the threshold away from all possible sanity: the by-product effects of the indicated level of launch of attack reach the state of likelihood of a general extinction of the human species. The only hypothetical case under which any power would seek to do what President Barack Obama has postured as his intention, would be a program of unbridled acceleration from mass-murder, into human extinction. That, as a mission-intention, could only exist under the condition that the leader of the nation which would launch such warfare were clinically insane personally, or that he, or she would prefer to bring on human extinction, rather than submit to humanly rational behavior.

Since the only public presentation of a treatment of such implications, is that of President Barack Obama, the question posed is clearly that either (a.) Barack Obama is only bluffing; (b.) that he is clinically insane; or, (c.) that, given the role of our Federal Constitution respecting war, he is prepared to destroy the human species, unless his Emperor-Nero-like fantasies are the ruling consideration for him personally. Adolf Hitler, anyone?

That much said respecting Obama as such, a less commonplace version of the same paradoxical predicament in policy-shaping follows.

The SDI Outlook Considered

Thus, certain matters should have become clear, since the first, 1983, rejection of U.S. President Ronald Reagan's backing for a Strategic Defense Initiative (SDI), a rejection which had become "hardened," with the approaching election of the administration under President George H.W. Bush. The trend in U.S. and related strategic policy-outlook since 1983, has been a commitment of both the witting and the witless to the pathway toward thermonuclear extermination, one which President Barack Obama now brings to the brink of systemic virtual human extermination now. One must never put "practical politicians" in charge of serious strategic decision-making again! You need not defeat them as readily as they will ruin themselves with their own "practical way of scheming;" but, you must defeat them, in any case. Unfortunately, such "practical schemers" as those, may bring about the destruction of everyone with their "practical way of scheming," as we witness precisely that sort of suicidal "cleverness" among our scheming "practical political authorities" of much of our present U.S. leadership of today, particularly those reckless and cowardly folk who will not resist the re-election of the current President.

Now, look back, again, to the resistance to President Ronald Reagan's attempts at reaching an "SDI" agreement during his two successive terms in office. We should recall how stupid the cleverness of some "practical politicians," such as Reagan's leading opponents in this matter, can turn out to have been. Looking back to then, from here, in the meantime, as I had warned repeatedly since 1983, we had come to experience the fall and subsequent break-up of the Soviet Union which I projected (in 1983) to occur "within about five years," as that should have been recognized even in 1983, as coming under then continuing trends which had been set into motion by, as I had forecast during 1983, "about 1988."

The Fall of the Soviet Union

As I had foreseen, and had warned repeatedly since the "SDI" initiative in which I played a certain keystone role leading into 1983, the fall of the Soviet Union was used immediately, with the fall of the East Germany "DDR," the subsequent Polish crisis, and the sequel of 1991, as the occasion to launch the destruction of the sovereignty of the nations of *both* continental western and central Europe. This change was prompted by the threats uttered by France's Socialist President François Mitterrand, against Germany at that time, and was implemented on the entirety of western and central continental Europe by the order of Britain's Prime Minister Margaret Thatcher and U.S. President George H.W. Bush (the son of the one-time supporter of the career of Adolf Hitler, Prescott Bush). It was that action by Mitterrand et al., in concert with Britain's Margaret Thatcher, and wobbly U.S. President George H.W. Bush, who had created, then, the mess which is the hyperinflationary disintegration of western and central continental Europe presently—into a threatened new "Schachtian" model for a hyperinflationary hoax of pretended "economic resurrection."

However, the preconditions for what Mitterrand did to destroy Western Europe, as we see the remains of that today, had been aided through U.S. complicity, that specifically of U.S. President George H.W. Bush, then squatting in London, in supporting the London-France destruction of the sovereignties of what had been the sovereign states of Western Europe through threats of military action delivered via Mitterrand's France. Thus,

the destruction of the sovereignties of Eastern Europe has served as the lever for the destruction of Western Europe, and now, with President Barack Obama, the system of nation-states of the world at large.

This was a ruinous action in willful violation of the Westphalian Principle, effected with aid of the complicity of President George H.W. Bush,[5] of the western and central European continent, which has been conducted under the pretext of establishing a "Euro system," a system under which all the nations of western and central Europe would be undergoing a systemic kind of thorough-going, "post-Westphalian" extinction of the residue of their past sovereignties. In the meanwhile, more and more under the recent nearly a dozen years, as under the obscenity of the George W. Bush, Jr. and Obama administrations, during the global process of, especially, the trans-Atlantic region, the course of strategic history has converged at an accelerating rate, toward a London-directed, but U.S.-conducted intention for the extinction of not only the region of western Asia, but the threatened thermonuclear extinction of Russia, China, and others: all of this has been, so far, intended in favor of a one-world empire in the heritage of what had once been the Roman Empire, an intended world empire of not much more than, at most, about a billion persons, mostly stupefied echoes of the most brutal of ancient oligarchical cults.

In summary on this subject of the European crisis at this present time, the selected means for imposing such an intention, was the precondition of the absolute supremacy for the conduct of thermonuclear exterminations. Therefore, the policy of neither peace nor war, for as long as possible, between the United States' party, and that of Russia and its party. Actual warfare would mean the ultimate consequence of the virtual extinction of all relevant parties.

Would it be, as the poet spoke, that "with this regard, their currents turn awry, and lose the name of action…"?[6]

That much said; return to the case of scientist Edward Teller's participation in the August 20-23, 1983 proceedings at Erice, Italy.[7] Turn to the still present, still strategically crucial issue of the SDI and my personal role in this continuing strategic process.

---

5. And, thus, implicitly his relevant violation of the U.S. Federal Constitution, while serving as U.S. President.

6. Wm. Shakespeare, **Hamlet**, Act III. Scene 1

7. See http://www.larouchepub.com/eiw/public/1983/eirv10n34-19830906/eirv10n34-19830906_016-beam_weapons_strategy_relaunched.pdf

How did those SDI-centered events of the early 1980s come about? How had I come to emerge as a significant factor in the course of what was to be a leading factor in that moment of world history since the Autumn of 1977? How did I happen to become the pivotal figure in the process, leading from my U.S. Presidential election-campaign of 1976, into the time when the U.S. Presidency of President Ronald Reagan had held victory for mankind briefly in his hands in 1983? For President Reagan, this was no stunt, but a commitment to which he remained devoted throughout his terms in office, and even his commitment to the belief that, even later than that, the proposed "SDI" must be realized at some foreseeable future time.

Between my commitments on the matter of economic policies, commitments which I had developed during processes going into the matter of the deep recession of the late 1950s, I have been a uniquely successful economic forecaster of that time, and was to be recognized, in fact, as a leading forecaster of the period of the 1971 crisis, and beyond; so, there had been a process in motion which led through the Strategic Defense Initiative (SDI) of the late 1970s and early 1980s.[8]

This was not a matter of an isolated event, or events. It was a "living process" which has continued to exist since those times, through to the present date. Consider some obscured actual roots of my part in what became later expressed as obscured but essential elements of seeds of later flourishing history.

Back during the 1956-1957 interval, I had been a rising influence within my own territory of corporate operations, in my then rising role as an executive of a management consulting organization, up to that time. During the latter part of that time, in the meantime, I

Lawrence Livermore National Laboratory

President Reagan awards the National Medal of Science to Dr. Edward Teller in 1983. Teller's efforts on behalf of the SDI and his mission to protect mankind from the threat of asteroid impacts, LaRouche writes, represent the quality of humanity in science demanded of us today.

had received several approaches from the FBI of that "period," approaches which had begun with an agent's projected actions which I regarded as in the nature of "silly filibustering," and which I explained in some concise terms to the FBI agent who approached me with his proposal for cooperation.

The FBI then decided to "punish" me, by measures which included, in effect, the break-up of my marriage to a wife who believed the lies of her wrong friends, and, later, a period of extended unpleasantnesses extended into the Spring 1968 political eruption at Columbia University, and affairs beyond, even internationally. The change in the quality and scale of my influences here and abroad, came at the onset of the August 1971 collapse of the economic policies of the existing monetarist system under President Richard Nixon, which suddenly changed things for me on an increasingly grander scale, later reaching even trans-oceanic dimensions.[9]

It happened that I had been the only publicly known

____

8. Ed. Note: Pivotal was LaRouche's debate with leading Keynesian economist, Abba Lerner, at Queens College, Dec. 2, 1971, where he so exposed Lerner's fascist policies, that the latter's colleagues determined they would never give LaRouche the chance for such a public debate again.

____

9. It is sometimes rightly said, that who you do is more significant than what you do. For me, personally and otherwise, that is not a quip; it is my personal history in today's world at large. Sometimes, implications are the most significant of all practical facts.

EIRNS/Stuart Lewis

Lyndon LaRouche announces his independent Presidential campaign at a press conference on July 19, 1984, in San Francisco. His mobilization for the SDI was a focal point of that campaign, and of his bid earlier that year for the Democratic Presidential nomination.

economist who had presented an actually competent forecast of the major financial crisis of the U.S. economy over the course of the 1968-1971 period. This development brought a significant change in my status internationally. Within the U.S. itself, I had been the only relatively well-known economist at that time (especially in the New York City region and somewhat beyond) who had forecast the exact kind of economic crisis which had struck in August 1971. Those facts were widespread, and also irrefutable in fact.

Many seeds cast in history remain merely seeds. Others become history. The seed, in my personal case, was an exceptionally successful economic forecast of a major recession, one which would soon disrupt the U.S. economy severely with an economic crisis which struck suddenly in the automobile and related industries in the February-March 1957 "deep recession" of the late 1950s. My method of economic forecasting was suddenly confirmed, whereas the statistical methods still in vogue today, had failed, suddenly and persistently, for that past time, and more emphatically, now. The same issue was expressed on a far broader and deeper scale, in President Richard Nixon's relative economic break-

down-crisis of early August 1971. Suddenly, in the late Summer of 1971, the unique quality of my successes as an economic forecaster since 1956, seemed to explode into virtually global directions over the remaining months leading into a globally publicized, December 2, 1971 debate, in which I was the relevant principal in the matter of those international crises which had suddenly seized the imagination as a leading factor in the economic process of the preceding months. The effects of that have never diminished but for brief intervals, with new crises kindling the old fires into often still greater dimensions. History is fairly often like that, especially during intervals of widespread economic or related forms of crises.

As was said of the alleged kicking of a cow in Chicago, small beginnings sometimes have gigantic consequences, even if they were merely rumors.

The root of that development in my case is to be traced, in turn, back to my forecast which I had first presented formally in August 1956: the most serious recession of the period, which, I warned, must almost certainly tend to erupt by February-March 1957.[10] Other executives of the consulting firm bureaucracy in disagreement with me, emphatically, at that time, and later, based their stubborn rejection of my forecast as premised on admiration for "statistical forecasting methods," which I warned would be entirely irrelevant for this case. The crisis broke out during the end of February 1957, and earliest March. What I had foreseen was now changing everything in the economy at that moment.

There had been nothing unusual in the opposition to my forecast. It happened that the methods of forecasting used by my rivals in that firm, were based chiefly on deductive statistical methods, which I knew were then, as now, always wrong, and also, usually, intrinsically incompetent, then, as now; but they also expressed prevalent popular opinion among economists of those, as also still present times. What had begun during the second half of the 1950s, did not end there; it came back to the surface beginning in early 1968. Meanwhile, there had been a crucial change, during a brief several years,

---

10. A specific factor of timing predetermined by the influence of credit-system factors specific to those industries. A relevant, but later reform of the contract relations between the industries and the automobile dealerships, was of crucial significance for the industry's credit practices.

toward an economic renaissance which had intervened during the course of what were to be merely several years of the U.S. Presidency under John F. Kennedy.

Why Economists Usually Fail

Then, as now, the prevailing incompetence exhibited by most of those considered as qualified economists, is a reflection of the accounting doctrine's influence on forecasting the future in no other aspect but that of extrapolation enhanced by cheating the credulous. The failure which that method inherently represents, is illustrated by the case of every competent discovery of a previously undiscovered principle. The effect of that problem runs as follows.

Consider every class of living creature excepting mankind. Those creatures are characterized by the inability to discover a new physical principle. Thus, the great majority of all living creatures, excepting mankind, are condemned to ultimate extinction, unless mankind enables them to outflank such a tragic destiny. Mankind, who exhibits the relevant point in the most convenient modes, is the only known living creature which actually chooses to use fire as an essential basis for its existence. This function of fire is locatable in the specifically noëtic characteristic of the human species, the characteristic which separates mankind as superior to every other known variety of living species.

It happens, that no true invention of a principle of nature can be derived from what can be specifically defined as deductive. In other words, Sherlock Homes relied upon drug addictions, otherwise, a creature of his specific nature could never imagined that he had deduced a principle of nature. The manner in which the accounting systems are obliged to function in respect to calculations, tends to ensure that, only in rare cases, are trained economists competent in the actualities of the scientific progress on which the sustaining and advancement of the physical economy of nations and their cultures absolutely depend. Thus, the typical "environmentalist" of today, is also functionally insane in precisely this particular sense of the matter.

In the actual history of economies, the most crucial distinction is to be found in an estimated ration of a human population, even at pre-school levels of education, who have become habituated in a significant degree to a form of noëtic development which foreshadows the creative Classical artistic and physical scientist of the adolescent and adult levels of development. It is, therefore, of great importance, to estimate the ration of the employable adolescent and adult populations which are properly identified as "creative," or, to choose a more rigorous terminology, noëtic development. I mean, the discovery of new principles of nature, principles of a categorical type which include Classical modes of artistic composition and related expression.

It is the rate of incidence, development, and progress, in those specifically noëtic modes of scientific and Classical-artistic expression in the young, and in the ration of employment of persons of those types, which tends to pre-determine the ability of societies to generate a combination of Classical-artistic and physical-scientific development and expression which is indispensable for preventing a society from degenerating into a direction of its collapse for reason of stagnant trends in habits. Thus, just the typical monetarist accountant, such as the Wall Street types, may be vigorous in his active practice, but his adopted nature is to produce a net less-than-nothing of real value devoted to the purposes of promoting the welfare of mankind.

The cases of the two categories of banking supply illustration of this point. The banker who is engaged with good conscience, must rely upon the progress, including significant noëtic progress, of both the banker's clients and also a supply of a quality of clientele which is engaged in physical-creative growth of scientifically progressive increase of the productive powers of labor.

The investment banker may sometimes take the same course of action, to which I would have no objection as along as he stays in his particular neck of the economic woods. With such honest investment bankers, the Obama administration's cronies of Obama's Geithner, would prefer to have nothing to do; their own company would, therefore, not be missed by actually respectable investment bankers. No honest and also intelligent banker would wish to be associated, or consign his children to the custody of a society ruled by a President Barack Obama. Indeed competent bankers, including those among investment bankers, will be moving in droves toward seeking the safe-harbor which Glass-Steagall uniquely affords.

Similarly, a so-called "green policy for economy" is inherently a recipe for mass death-rates within any society which accepts such a standard of practice. It is only the increase of the energy-flux density of physically productive increase of per-capita physical output, which stands between society and increased death-rates in societies. (Human life can not stand still.) This point is the same, in respect to such effects, as the defense of the continued existence of the human species on our planet and also beyond. The need of means for defending our own planet, requires us to adopt responsibility for our planet's own neighborhood.

Kennedy and Clinton

The interval of the John F. Kennedy administration had seen a reversal of the trend of which I had warned during 1966-71 and beyond. However, the burying of the truth of the Kennedy assassination, plunged the United States into a trend of economic decline which has been continued, in fact, during the entire span of U.S. national history since the moment the "cover up" of the Kennedy assassination had been put into play. That led into the fall of President Richard Nixon and the following interim of the late 1970s. With the still later defeat of the initiative for the SDI and the subsequent, disgusting performance of President George H.W. Bush, the U.S.A. slid into a perpetual economic decline, ever since, to the present date.

However, during the short life of the Kennedy Presidency, a curiously ironical fact had crossed my path. It was the name of a young fellow from Arkansas, "Bill" Clinton, who turned up as a name among a group of apparent admirers of President Kennedy. One must be careful in reporting history!

In the meantime, other things had happened. The election, and later years in office of President William Jefferson Clinton had been a factor of relative stabilization, up to the launching of the campaign for the attempt to impeach him. Nonetheless, during the Clinton years, there were important developments up through the point of the attempted impeachment; but, there was no reversal of what continued to be an actually accelerating decline toward collapse in the U.S. and European economies.

President Clinton had attempted to address the economic crisis, if in a limited, but constructive way, coming out of the Summer of 1998 into the political catastrophe dumped into his lap during the Autumn; but, otherwise, he had done nothing to reverse the continuing process of economic decline of the U.S. economy which had been set into motion, originally, by the effect of the assassinations of President John F. Kennedy and John's brother and Presidential pre-candidate Robert Kennedy. Since President Clinton's retirement from office, the U.S. economy has been careening along a course of national economic disintegration. With this approaching Autumn, the apparent prospect for the U.S.A. is that of nothing as much as pure destruction, even something much worse, unless President Obama is soon placed "on the skids."

I shall now shift the course of the report to the subject of the principles which have shaped European and trans-Atlantic shaping of history, up to the verge of the present dates.

II. Against Oligarchical Principles

In the course of what has come to be identified as "European history," some among us who are the proud bearers of the tradition of the "European cultural vintage," have come to converge on the notion of an Homeric account of the fall of the criminally butchered city-state of Troy. Whatever the weak points of the available, historical accounts, the fact remains, that European civilization has been dominated, at least for most of the rather reasonably known times, by the persistence of what is known as "The Oligarchical System." We, whether Europeans, or with their nominal descendants in the Americas, for example, have continued to be dominated by the tradition of that Mediterranean-pivoted oligarchical system, which is now principally associated with the social-political imagery associated with the descent of the Roman empire.

The view contrary to my own, that of the so-called "Greenie" or "Environmentalist" traditions, is a product of the oligarchical principle as that has been traced, from the Homeric legacy, to the oligarchical system which is, with relatively rare exceptions, usually employed in common definition of both ordinary and extraordinary human minds, alike. The former populations tend to be classed, in some instances, as a talking variety of what are seemingly like virtually mere cattle, or, better said, virtually the type of foolish slave who forges his own shackles, shackles which he often installs as a kind of habit, to serve him as the predator ravishing his own mind.

Those human beings who are stubbornly disinclined to bear a slave's submission to an oligarchical rule, as typified by the case of the American Revolutionaries who fought against the oligarchical legacy of those persons who are like willing slaves, like those who, even habitually, wear the shackles of a New Venetian party of that William of Orange, et al., who was the typical adversary of the great cultural achievements of the Massachusetts Bay settlement of the Winthrops and Mathers, must be considered against the background of such elements of post-Troy history generally.

The temporary crushing of what was to become our later United States, must also be examined for its value as among lessons of history, lessons which include what are still threatened to be imposed upon them according to the rule of the same oligarchical tradition of evil which slaughtered the Christians on behalf of the principle of the Roman empire, or such as the Jews under Adolf Hitler's following. Take the evil tyrannies, which are rooted in that oligarchical tradition which is presently named as the "Greenies," for example, or the Roman mass-murders of Christians in the arena or otherwise. These episodes in history happen, and have always lurked in the shadows of even the greatest human endeavors, unless we are sufficiently armed and alert to prevent such insurgencies of evil.

"A greenie," for example, who adopts his, or her code of practice, may be not only a slave in his or her own right, but a slave who tends to commit atrocities against those who do not inflict slavery upon themselves, as on others. So, the "Greenie's" habits have become increasingly a menace to the continued existence of the human species in a general way.

The physical evidence which supplies the proof for my argument here, is efficiently locatable in a contrast of what are fairly called "normal members" of the human species, to the beasts generally. The essential distinction of the human species in its healthy, normal state, is defined as human in its typical behavior, as I have noted in the preceding chapter of this report, defined by a habit of a willful reliance upon a principle of increase of relative energy-flux density, as opposed to the bestiality common to all species other than mankind. The qualified, apparent exception to that propensity for slaughter, is to be found in the training of breeds of animal species, in those practices prompted, essentially, by human training of specimens of animal varieties, as under conditions of animal husbandry. There is, thus, an increasing tendency toward limiting the cultivation of animal species to those species and types whose induced behavior is not inconvenient for mankind.

The distinction of mankind from beasts, including emphasis in favor of specifically cultivated varieties, is precisely that. I recapitulate, in a fresh form, what I have written on this account earlier, as a needed preliminary note.

Now Consider 'Fire'

The crucial test of that distinction of man from beast, is located in the uniqueness of the human personality with respect to that of all other, known forms of life. We might therefore speak, truthfully: of the creative intellect which is specific to the human species. It were better, to make the distinction of the human species from other species, by beginning with a practical choice of an alternate approach to describing a standard: *mankind's progress in the mastery of fire—increase in energy-flux density across the boundaries which mark the birth of successive generations of the culture of a successful form of organized society.*[11] That means, as I have repeatedly treated the subject in earlier locations, a distinction consistent with the notion of an order of rank among distinct species of both the qualities and the applications of fire. In fact, the notion of the principled order of the definitions of "fire" is coherent with the orderable notion of "value," as "value" is to be located in the hierarchical-like ordering of relatively lower, to reach higher physical states of matter, as these changes are employed as policies of practice by human societies.

Herein lies an exact distinction of man from beast, or man's organized, willful progress in development of practice, from relatively lower "energy-flux densities," to higher.

This brings us back to what must follow from a related argument presented in the immediately preceding chapter of this present report.

The Creative Mentality Defined

For example, mankind's science is currently progressing from ordinary combustion, through, successively, thermonuclear fusion and matter-antimatter reactions. This represents a state of human scientific progress associated, typically, at root, with the inseparable categories of (1) physics, and (2) of the Classical musical qualifications of Max Planck and Albert Einstein, and the general principle of mind associated with the achievements of (3) Planck's collaborator Wolfgang Köhler, creating thus a set of principles respecting the still scarcely known, deeper principles of the human mind. Each and all of these "factors" urgently need to be understood as matters of principle.

The most crucial issues, at this stage of the history

---

11. Many forms of society have existed which were, or still are, inherently defective, the oligarchical models most notably.

NASA/JPL-Caltech

The successful landing of the rover Curiosity on Mars gives mankind hope of organizing an effective defense of Earth against asteroid impacts and other threats from space. Shown is a "self-portrait" of the deck of the rover from its navigation camera, showing the rim of Gale Crater, the lighter strip of land in the background.

process connecting points of "broadcast" of functional platforms on Mars to the speed of light exchanged between Earth and Mars. Factors come into play, thus, such that we can no longer tolerate the notion that the human intellect is an extension of the function of an array of sense-perceptions per se: when we must admit that it is the process of transmission itself, which enables us to define the process as a whole. Fourteen minutes difference has a crucially subsuming role, especially when we take into consideration the implications of the need to master control over the masses of asteroid-like aggregations which contain the threats to Earth and the like from the asteroids converging on destinies such as targeting of mankind's refuge known to us as "Earth."

Our objective must be to attempt to gain such forms of control of that apparent debris which could end up as mines in space for the complex of Earth and Moon which might be gathered to our future advantage there.

In that process, and related matters, the included objective is to free mankind from that superstition which is known as "sense perception." The important thing might be, indeed, "the effect;" but, more important is "that which generates the apparent effect." Our objective should be to discover how to gain increasing "leverage" in so-called "space" in control of the processes which include the rubble in the space-volumes from Mars-orbit to Jupiter-orbit.

Now, to clarify the point I had introduced above, return attention to the matter of mind-as-such, as presented by Köhler to Max Planck, and as adopted by Planck. I have met very little beyond bare-bones evidence which reaches to the crucial aspects of Köhler's core-argument. This may well be among the effects left behind by the sequence of so-called "World War I," and the lunatic characteristics of the influence of such as Bertrand Russell's role in the scientific debates and cultisms of the post-World War I 1920s. Whatever the

of such processes, pertain to the errors associated with popular views respecting the principles of human comprehension. The worst aspect of the short-falls in even the practice of scientific principles today, are those associated with the widely popular, but incompetent notions respecting "human sense-certainty." This problem is one which I recently addressed in my "Next, Beyond Mars,"[12] in which I dealt with the critical issue of communications implicitly confronting us with the success of the presently new, crucially ironical phase of the developments presented to us implicitly by the results of "Curiosity's" progress so far.

As I have emphasized in an earlier report, when we consider the specific advances in sophistication incorporated in the design and deployment of "Curiosity," we should consider ourselves impelled to recognize a certain important bit of irony. This means, to deprecate the attempt to correlate the functions of the human mind with sense-perception as such, and to shift attention to the implications of the transmission of what is called "information" when the transmission is located as a

---

12. See *Feature* in this issue, or LaRouche PAC (http://larouchepac.com/node/23679).

case adduced from such latter sources, the general point which the Köhler-Planck discussion presents, is that all human knowledge is a category of the essentially indivisible, that to such effect that the mind is to be considered as conditionally partitioned, but not categorically. It is we, in effect, who partition knowledge between experiences, rather than accreting separatable categories of experiences. We are, so to speak, responsible for assimilating a defensible conception into a continuity of a unified idea.

That suggests that we distinguish the nameable "tag" such as a name from the substance to which that "tag" has been attached. The ontological actual essence of the idea as such, is distinguished from that which is the named shadow of the "tag." Thus, the substance of human thought, is thus distinguishable in degree from the name given to an adopted "objective" aspect of the process to be considered. This comes directly to the surface in the experience of the recovery of a previously familiar name-likeness of an actually relevant process of thought—as if in recall of an interrupted memory, which remains knowable, if its recovery is properly motivated with respect to the entirety of the domain.

This is a typical sort of ordinary problem, as in either recalling old names or recognizing that which is to be named.

The crucial significance of all considerations along these lines, can not be efficiently separated from the implications of the discovery of a new concept—one not known, or named before: a kind of synthesis of a new idea, rather than some sort of synonym: in new categories of discoveries corresponding to an independently original conception based on a previously unknown experience. This points in the direction of a true cognitive process. Significantly, the work of Planck and Einstein, especially in respect to the importance of Classical musical composition for both of them, as of Johann Sebastian Bach, or Wilhelm Furtwängler, brings the focus of our attention on "these implied connections."

Or, a more precisely defined notion to similar effect, is found in the pathological features of the reduction of ideas to the functional characteristics of the domain of fixed parts, as in playing the notes, rather than performing the actual music.

Edward Teller Remembered

Those among us who have shared some knowledge of the kinds of scientific mission-orientation underlying the launching of the Strategic Defense Initiative (SDI) and kindred missions, who share it more or less immediately, as I do, or as do younger persons committed to this same legacy, can not overlook what I recall as Dr. Edward Teller's leading contributions to what became known by both of us as "The Strategic Defense Initiative (SDI)." We must also focus a mission-orientation commitment to the defense of Dr. Teller's leading role in today's crucial goal of defending both the parts, and, ultimately, the whole of our planet Earth against what might be considered, in the rough, as "space debris."

At the same time, we recall with some touches of bitterness, that minds such as those of Max Planck and Albert Einstein point us toward leading thinkers from the generation of Max Planck and Albert Einstein who have represented something which tended to become lost in the course of what is recalled as "World War I" and post-"World War II" scientific and musical society. Much that had been beautiful as scientific achievement, became relatively mired in the cheap-shot qualities of practice which became all too familiar in the generation educated under post-World War II conditions. In effect, these, my own recollections, must also have often occurred to a qualified "Martian" such as my ironical sometime critic, Dr. Teller.

Dr. Teller is remembered with a particular emphasis on the subject of the SDI and today's increasing concern for the need of means of defense against asteroids which have been, are, or may be deadly threats to large parts of the population of Earth, or, ultimately, worse. Those of my associates now, recognize that a very serious concern is needed against this general threat, especially in light of our stunning lack of knowledge respecting the awesomely great mass of potentially threatening asteroids whose identities we have yet to locate.

All of this which I have just presented as content within this present chapter of the report, now separates the practice of science prior to "Curiosity," from the larger category which the success of "Curiosity" has prompted to be recognized as an entirely new and much greater pathway to be opened now, when the foothold of mankind on Mars has just gained an awesomely greater mission-objective in all conceivable respects. The particular mission to which Dr. Teller had devoted particular attention, the threat to man on Earth from asteroids, should be long remembered, together with his famous mustering of efforts on behalf of the Strategic Defense Initiative (SDI) as the quality of humanity in science which the present threat of thermonuclear warfare demands of us all today.

With that, will come a further, very special concern of my own: the true meaning of the human mind.